SIMPLY Splendid SUPPERS

JOHN TOVEY

BBC BOOKS

ACKNOWLEDGEMENTS

I could not have written this book without the continued indulgence of my staff at Miller Howe, or the loyal hard work and enthusiasm of Chris Blaydes. Chris joined us twelve years ago, straight from college, with a burning ambition to cook. He was difficult at times, and we had many horrendous rows and shows of temper. He got married some four years ago, and has even had to celebrate each anniversary away from Jo as they clash with our demonstrations around the country and at the farm in the Rossendale Valley.

I gave him complete control of the kitchen at Miller Howe in October 1994, and we have introduced his modern, light and full-of-flavour cooking, changing from five rich courses to four less rich courses, using heavily reduced stocks and strong vinaigrettes instead of fattening creams for sauces, and titillating the palate with a galaxy of flavours and interesting textures.

Whilst I was in the sunny Cape he did all the food involved in the photography for this book, and then came out to Johannesburg with the staff where we presented our Festival of British Country House Cooking there and in Cape Town itself.

I am sure that in the next decade he will have very much made his mark on the British culinary scene. I certainly wish him well and look forward to many more years of working alongside him. In his turn, he is very well looked after by Susan Elliot, his second, and the other members of the small kitchen team.

Published by BBC Books, an imprint of BBC Worldwide Publishing.
BBC Worldwide Limited, Woodlands, 80 Wood Lane, London W12 0TT

First published 1995

©John Tovey 1995
The moral right of the author has been asserted.

ISBN 0 563 37150 1

Edited by Susan Fleming.
Designed by Mason Linklater
Photographs by Chris Turner
Food preparation for photography by Chris Blaydes

Set in Garamond
Printed in Great Britain by Cambus Litho Ltd, East Kilbride
Bound in Great Britain by Hunter and Foulis Ltd, Edinburgh
Colour separations by Radstock Reproductions Ltd, Midsomer Norton
Jacket printed by Lawrence Allen Ltd, Weston-super-Mare

Contents

Introduction   4

Fresh Ingredients   5

Store-cupboard Ingredients   7

Starters   11

Main Courses   78

Vegetable Accompaniments   127

Desserts   148

Some Suggested Menus   190

Index   191

Introduction

I have loved food for more years than I care to remember – in my childhood it was very much part of the daily scene – and have been involved with actually cooking for 24 years here at Miller Howe. I also love entertaining at my farm, in the Rossendale Valley, and used to find myself working extremely hard from early morning in order to get an MGM production on the stage that evening, and then being faced with mountains of mess at the end. No longer.

These past three or four years have found me cutting down, but only on the number of courses and the type of menu. This immediately diminishes the amount of work involved beforehand, and reduces the slog afterwards. A lot of the dishes can be prepared or made the day before, or at least in the morning, which saves precious time on the evening itself. A lot of the dishes rely on the store-cupboard, which also cuts down to a certain extent on shopping time.

Splendidly successful supper parties, even if fairly informal, do need to be planned well in advance. This, too, will save you having panics on the evening itself. Try to have as much of the food as possible prepared before the evening: most of the recipes tell you when you can do what. To give an example, take my first suggested menu on page 190. The Bolognese, Mustard Dressing and Chocolate Walnut Torte (don't fill the latter, though), could all be made the day before and stored as appropriate until needed. The starter dishes could be brought together on the morning of your party, as could the batter for the fish. On the evening itself, you can slice and fill the torte. Then, when ready to eat, you cook and eat the starter, and then deep-fry the fish at the very last minute. I think you'll agree that that doesn't involve too much work!

Try, too, to have as much general organisation done in advance as possible. If you're coming home from outside for supper – from the theatre or ballet, perhaps – your guests will be gratified by the sight of a laid table with silver and crystal gleaming, and flowers in place. Even if you have a half-hour of cooking still to do, they'll be persuaded that you are properly in control if they are greeted by a bottle of chilled wine and a bowl of olives, or something to nibble!

The following simple supper dishes are mostly just that in terms of *work*, but are still thoroughly enjoyed by diners, and are packed with flavour. Gone are the pounds of butter and pints of double cream I used to use, which now are substituted by healthy and flavourful oils and less fatty dairy foods. Visually, I still want dishes to *look* tempting, and obviously the palates of my guests must be titillated.

Halfway through testing and trying out these recipes, I suddenly realised how much I was enjoying myself, and finding that many of the dishes can be made in about 15 minutes. I was then struck with the horrible thought that this wasn't quite my image, but once you've read the book and tested the recipes yourself, I truly hope that the length of time you spend in your kitchen is much reduced, allowing you, like me, to catch up on *other* things you want to do rather than work.

Making up a two-course supper menu from the following recipes should not be difficult. Neither is it impossible to work out a three-course menu if you want to push the boat out (see my suggestions on page 190). Some of the starters could be expanded to make a main course, by adding a vegetable, and often a starter followed by a pud would make a perfectly adequate supper. These simple recipes, **all serving four people**, should find you enjoying the whole evening just as much as the guests, and capable of facing the clearing up once they have departed.

However, what have not changed are the *basic* ingredients. You can never spend too much time seeking out small and good suppliers near you. Good basics allied to a little skill will produce stunning results. I wish you joy!

FRESH INGREDIENTS

I no longer do everything by the book and, with hand on heart, tell my guests that everything is fresh. I have become a canny shopper, but I must admit to sadness concerning the demise of those super corner shops and speciality food outlets. In my valley alone, over 30 registered butchers have closed in these past four years, slaughterhouses which have been in the same family for decades are now defunct due to the onslaught of the

bureaucrats in Brussels. Smokers, cheese-makers, and endless others, honest, hard-working folk, face bankruptcy as mean 'standards' are introduced throughout this modern Europe. It might be what *they* call standards, but they bear no relationship to the true, old-fashioned, traditional standards in this country, that have been handed down from generation to generation. At the same time the supermarkets are trying their damnedest to improve standards and keep prices reasonable – in their terms, that is – but often prices are so unreasonable for producers that they are forced to throw in the towel.

At the hotel we *do* try and buy every item of produce such as meat, fish, fruit and vegetables as fresh as possible from as many local people as possible. Mr and Mrs Wild valiantly toil on their small-holding in Winster, and each year I can't wait for their spinach to be ready. As for their tomatoes...they are to die for. I always laugh when supermarkets sport shelf after shelf of various tomatoes and then suddenly show a few labelled, 'Grown for Flavour'. Why *else* should they be grown! The Wilds' tomatoes perfume the kitchen the very moment their stalks are plucked. These I never skin as there is so much flavour in this part of the fruit, and hardly a day goes by in the season that I don't have them thinly sliced, dribbled with French dressing and sprinkled with chopped fresh basil.

My local butcher in Crawshawbooth rears most of his meat and slaughters it on the farm, but the new legislation has added greatly to the cost of this service – in an attempt, we all believe, to prevent this type of killing. In the late summer he encourages local old-age pensioners with small gardens and allotments to sell their produce in his shop – truly a service that endears him to most of the villagers. A local baker who will sell you fresh yeast must be a gentleman. A fishmonger who will skin or scale should be encouraged. A local market trader selling only four or five cheeses made locally has to be used rather than the large outlets selling the cheaper polystyrene muck often sold as cheese but which resembles the soles of leather-cum-cardboard shoes. Milkmen who actually deliver and take note of your notes left in the empties have to be supported. Whenever possible, it is up to *us* to seek out and encourage such folk.

Most towns have their own local food markets, varying in degree of quality and choice. If the one nearest to you disappoints, ask, seek and find one that will please *you*. One of my favourite markets is Bury – close to my church – and I am always amazed at the seemingly never-ending stalls, all selling similar products and, more confusing still, all very close to one another. After several years, I now know who sells what suits me best in the vegetable, fish and fresh meat lines.

but must always be bought fresh. How often, though, can you get runny cheeses in supermarkets, in a good enough condition that they can be served the same day? (My solution to the problem of ripe Brie is on page 58.) Dolcelatte Torte has to be my very favourite of imported cheeses, but I also like and use Bel Paese, Roquefort, goat cheeses, and cream and curd cheeses such as Boursin and the Italian Mascarpone. However, there are many lovely folk in this country making their own in spite of every possible opposition from Brussels, so again, do please try and seek out their products.

Parmesan must always be bought in a whole wedge, never already grated. It sounds expensive when you see how much you have to pay for what seems so little, but it does go a long way.

One of the last jobs I do when leaving the farm for the hotel is to check my cheese stocks, and if in doubt I put the leftovers into a food processor, add a little freshly grated nutmeg and a glass of port, and then pot it and put it in the fridge. It is always commented on favourably when I serve it the following week!

DAIRY PRODUCTS

Things like cheeses, creams and yoghurt should be bought fresh too. As I've said, I now tend to use *crème fraîche* and *fromage frais* instead of double cream with everything! The former contains a third less butterfat than double cream, and has an interesting, slightly acid flavour; *fromage frais*, a fresh curd cheese, has much less fat, from 1–8 per cent, as opposed to over 40, and is wonderful used in cooking and as a garnish.

Cheeses, too, can be a bit of a problem,

STOCK

Another item that I keep for a short while in the fridge (or freezer) is stock. There's always something that I could use to make a stock, such as bones, spices and vegetables, and it will form the basis for a soup or a sauce. But supermarkets now sell stock in cartons, and often it's very good indeed – very time-saving. I don't find them quite strong enough in flavour though, so I always boil them to reduce them a little before use.

STORE-CUPBOARD INGREDIENTS

When I was a child, I remember going with my grandmother round the outside markets on Wednesdays and Saturdays just as they were closing, and I learned so much about what to look for in fresh produce. You must now, unfortunately, apply the same canniness to tinned, packeted and frozen produce. There are prawns and prawns, tomatoes and tomatoes. More often than not the price indicates which will be the superior product, but this is not always the case. When you find an item that pleases your palate – and to some extent your pocket as well – go for it!

Part of the success of simple supper entertaining at home depends on having a well-stocked store-cupboard. You can buy the major fresh ingredients of the meal – the meat, fish or vegetable – fresh on the day (or the day before if it has to be pre-prepared in some way), but for calm, unflustered cooking, it's best to have in a few sensible basics.

FROZEN FOODS

In the freezer I might keep some stock (see left), but I'm very rarely without frozen prawns, spinach, some fresh yeast, and some bought or home-frozen raspberries. The spinach can be used in a variety of ways, and the rasps can be eaten as they are (as a reminder of warmer weather), or puréed to make a sweet sauce (see page 179).

Buying frozen prawns is quite often a con. A bag will clearly state '1½ lb' in large bold type but, underneath, needing a magnifying glass to read it, will be a further message, 'including ½ lb frozen brine'. You must seek out a type of prawn which suits your own pocket and palate, and make sure they are absolutely defrosted before use. I buy prawns from my butcher – yes! – and they're large, superb, succulent and really taste of fish (Sambrand, I think they're Icelandic).

I bring frozen prawns out of the freezer *the day before*, and put what I need into the fridge. I then spread them out on a baking tray for a couple of hours in the kitchen, pour off any liquid, then finish them off by lightly tapping them with a double thickness of kitchen paper. They must be *thoroughly* defrosted and dry.

PACKETS

I'm assuming you will already have a selection of flours (plain white, strong white, self-raising, wholemeal and corn-flour), cereals like porridge oats, and several types of sugar (I use caster, granulated, soft brown, demerara, icing and cube). Other necessities for me are dried pasta (so easy to turn into a quick and good supper dish – see one idea on page 43), chocolate, chocolate digestive biscuits, powdered gelatine, bicarbonate of soda and a selection of teas, particularly Earl Grey (which I use in a couple of recipes, see pages 158 and 178).

Dried *porcini*, or ceps, are quite often found now, not just in Italian delis, and they're very handy. Soak them in warm water for at least half an hour, and then wash gently to get rid of any grit. Keep and strain the soaking liquid as it will contain a lot of the essential flavours of the mushrooms.

The other 'in thing' these days is the sun-dried tomato, which comes in all shapes, sizes and forms. I joined this bandwagon years ago, although I didn't take to them at first. When I lived in Nyasaland in the 1950s, a friend there used to dry her surplus tomatoes on top of her outbuildings on a Heath Robinson cane-guard draped with mosquito netting. The strong African sun used to dry the tomatoes in a few days, but they were not brilliantly tasty. However, now, after years of experimenting and tasting, and although it might sound terribly grand, I import my sun-dried tomatoes in bulk from the sunny Cape in tightly packed vacuum packs. These are put in the cellar and, when needed, are simply emptied into gallon plastic containers and covered with the Italian olive oil we use. I adore them and can't keep away from the ruddy containers. I prefer them in this state but occasionally, for a pasta dish, Chris (the head chef at Miller Howe) pours hot white wine over them and uses them the same day. It is definitely cheaper to buy them in the dried state, and then you can add whatever oil, vinegar and spice you personally like.

A selection of packeted whole or ground nuts, pine kernels and seeds like sesame, caraway and poppy are handy, and they can be used in a variety of ways. I'm also very keen on dried and glacé fruits. Always buy the very best you can afford, as the taste will be well worth it. Glacé fruits are now imported from the Cape, and they are wonderful.

SPICES AND FLAVOURINGS

I keep a small selection of whole and ground spices, which are always at hand to add piquancy, heat or colour when needed. Don't buy too much at a time,

though, as ground spices quickly lose their oomph. I use peppercorns a lot (black, white *and* pink), freshly ground, and both coarse sea and runny salt.

I like to have whole nutmegs to grind fresh as and when needed, and coriander and cumin seeds which I can grind fresh in my mortar. Paprika, mixed spice, ground and whole cinnamon and ground ginger are useful too; I always try to have the latter in other forms as well, fresh root (keep in the fridge) and preserved ginger in syrup. I usually try to make my own curry essence, but a good curry powder and curry paste can add just that perfect finishing touch of flavour.

Garlic I prefer to use fresh, but I have recently come across a jar of garlic paste which is very good indeed (Brookerpaks). Some brands are very soapy but, again, experiment and see what is to your own personal taste. Otherwise, just make up the equivalent of what I specify by crushing peeled fresh garlic with a little salt.

Mustard is vital to me – English-made, English dry and a good coarse-grain variety – as are little jars of tomato paste and horseradish cream, which add colour and zip to any number of things.

The one thing I have discovered which makes me wish I had been using it all the time is the pure vanilla extract from Madagascar. Vanilla is the only fruit-bearing orchid, with each flower opening just for one day each year. Pollinated by hand, the pod requires intensive labour care for up to six months and it takes 5lb (2.25kg) of harvested pods to produce 1lb (450 g) of cured pods suitable for culinary use. Use vanilla pods themselves (great for vanilla sugar, custard and ice-cream), but when you want a quick vanilla flavour, use this extract. It's available by mail order from Lakeland Plastics, and once you've tried it, you will understand what I mean when I say, 'Never again will vanilla essence be seen in my store-cupboard or used in my cooking'!

TINS, JARS AND BOTTLES

Tinned tuna is always in my store-cupboard in various sized tins and flavourings. Once again you have to find the one you like. I prefer the tuna in soy oil to the brined one, but for sheer self-indulgence there is one with sweetcorn and garlic mayonnaise which is *sinful* in a toasted sandwich. Tins of anchovies are useful too.

I also always have a few tins of a famous brand name condensed beef consommé, in addition to jars of home-made from the hotel in the freezer. They're good with a touch of curry essence and sherry, topped with *fromage frais* for a light lunch, or useful with prawns and sun-dried tomatoes as in the recipe on page 26.

I'm sure also to find a tin of baked beans around: hardly *haute cuisine*, but very satisfying!

For years, I used to religiously skin my fresh tomatoes, peel and slowly cook the onions to make my own tomato sauce, but now I use Sainsbury's chopped tomatoes with basil (see page 39). This is so much more convenient and so much quicker. Once again I bought examples of several ranges of tinned tomatoes at first: some passed the quality test, but many were really revolting – watery, tasteless and, occasionally, with a sharp, slightly off, hint. Once you find a variety and make that pleases you, go for it.

I also have on hand for occasional use, golden syrup, apricots in syrup, and that wonderful natural chestnut purée – all good for making a last-minute pud.

Jars of capers keep well, as do gherkins and chutneys (preferably home-made, see page 42). Olives, usually stoned black, are always good, even if for just a canapé, but they make a wonderful spread, tapenade (see page 50). Bovril, Marmite and Worcestershire sauce are useful too, not to be sniffed at, as well as a few sweet things such as redcurrant jelly, honey and apricot jam.

The bottles in the drinks cabinet should always be looked to for their possibilities in the flavouring stakes. Any number of sauces would be enhanced by a little judicious addition of alcohol. I use cooking brandy and sherry, rum, Irish whiskey, dry white wine, Marsala, port and cider. I'm not averse either to pouring in a little liqueur such as Frangelico, peach schnapps or, my current favourite, Cape Velvet, the South African equivalent of Bailey's Irish Cream.

OILS AND VINEGARS

I have about seven different kinds of each at the farm, but I always buy in small bottles, as the shelf life, of oil particularly, is short.

I have pure virgin olive oil, but I never, ever use it just by itself, as the taste reminds me, however peculiar this sounds, of an oil extract I was forced to drink as a kid by the spoonful each Friday after the weekly bath! However, virgin olive oil has become as much a passion with some people as claret, and I believe there are a myriad flavours available, depending on where the olives have been grown, and on how they have been treated during the expressing of the oil.

Choose any oil you want to use to suit your own taste, preferably one that is rich in polyunsaturates. For most cooking I favour a mild or bland oil like sunflower; when you want to add spice, heat or taste, choose something relevant. For instance, although I make my own chilli oil (see below), I've come across a wonderful one, called pirri-pirri oil, which is very heatedly aromatic!

When you open a nutty oil – sesame, walnut or hazelnut – it should be stored with the top firmly secured in the fridge, and used as quickly as possible. These have wonderful flavours. Use sesame in oriental type cooking. The other nut oils I think are too delicious (and expensive) to use much in cooking, so I add them to French dressings. Do so minimally, as they are very strong in flavour.

Supermarkets often sell six to eight different *flavoured* oils on their shelves, but I prefer to do the flavouring at home. I buy an ordinary sunflower oil and have ready some 1lb (450 g) screw-top jars. In one I put 8 peeled cloves of garlic and then fill it up with oil. I do the same with 6 chillies in another, and 2 grated dessertspoons of root ginger in yet another. Each time you make an oil and vinegar dressing, you should always use different oils (and vinegars) so as to keep your palate sharp!

In the early days of Miller Howe we were given a vinegar culture in its crock, and it stood on a shelf close to the dish-washing machine. Each night any dregs of wine left in bottles being returned from the dining room were poured into the vinegar crock. It meant there was never any consistency of flavour or strength, but the satisfaction it gave me was great. Nowadays I basically use either a white or red wine vinegar, and occasionally a home-made raspberry (and even a malt in certain dishes). But the one that has taken the culinary scene by storm is balsamic. On a trip to New York a few years ago, in a posh food shop there were shelf-loads of the stuff in various sizes and varying shaped bottles at all sorts of prices. A small bottle of fourteen-year-old mature balsamic was on sale at a staggering price and, wanting to know if it was worth it, I bought one and carried it in my flight bag home to the Lake District as if it were gold. It was thicker in texture, softer in taste and lighter in aroma, but definitely not worth what I had paid.

When next you buy a small bottle of white wine vinegar, halfway through using it, stick in a couple of generous sprigs of rosemary and leave it for a month. You will be amazed at the new aroma it gives off. You can do the same with tarragon and mint – in fact the two mixed together make for a very unusually flavoured vinegar.

SIMPLY
Splendid
STARTERS

Beetroot
and
Orange
Cream
Soup
(page 15)

Banana
and
Parsnip
Cream
Soup
(page 14)

Apple,
Red Pepper
and
Sweetcorn
Cream Soup
(page 15)

CREAM SOUPS

I still use stock from the stockpot when entertaining for over eight folk, or when I have roasted chicken, game or a joint, but the following *quick* methods and combinations give four extremely large and filling portions of soup for supper. They're all creamy and very delicious.

Follow the basic method for every soup, adding the individually specified vegetables and/or fruit when appropriate (this varies a little). You don't have to peel or core the apples and pears when you use them, as they will be sieved later on.

BASIC METHOD

2 oz (50 g) soft butter

4 oz (100 g) onions, peeled and coarsely chopped

individual soup fruit or veg (see below)

4 tablespoons cooking sherry

1½ pints (900 ml) milk

salt and freshly ground black pepper

Melt the butter in a large pan, add the onion and gently fry for 15 minutes. Add the individual specified vegetables or fruit, along with the sherry, cover with doubled greaseproof paper and the lid, and cook on a very, very low heat for 40 minutes.

Add the milk, then liquidise. Sieve, and your soup is made. If reheating, do so very gently, then season to taste.

BANANA AND PARSNIP

12 oz (350 g) parsnips, trimmed, peeled and chopped

4 oz (100 g) banana, peeled and chopped

Add the parsnips to the onion and butter with the sherry, and cook for 40 minutes. Add the banana when liquidising.

PARSNIP AND PEAR

8 oz (225 g) parsnips, trimmed, peeled and chopped

8 oz (225 g) pears, chopped

Add both to the onion and butter with the sherry, and cook for 40 minutes.

BEETROOT AND ORANGE

12 oz (350 g) beetroots, peeled and finely chopped

5 fl oz (150 ml) fresh orange juice

2 level teaspoons ground cumin

Add the beetroot to the onion and butter with the sherry, and cook for 40 minutes. Add the orange juice and cumin, with only 1 pint (600 ml) milk, when liquidising.

APPLE, RED PEPPER AND SWEETCORN

4 oz (100 g) apples, chopped

6 oz (175 g) red peppers, seeded and chopped

6 oz (175 g) sweetcorn kernels, off the cob

Add all to the onion and butter with the sherry, and cook for about 40 minutes.

APPLE, CELERY AND MUSHROOM

6 oz (175 g) apples, chopped

4 oz (100 g) celery, chopped

6 oz (175 g) mushrooms

Add all to the onion and butter with the sherry, and cook for 40 minutes.

BROCCOLI AND CAULIFLOWER

12 oz (350 g) cauliflower, cut into small florets

4 oz (100 g) broccoli, cut into small florets

Add both to the onion and butter with the sherry, and cook for 40 minutes.

SPINACH AND TOMATO

6 oz (175 g) fresh spinach, tough stalks removed

12 oz (350 g) tomatoes, roughly chopped

Add both to the onion and butter with the sherry, and cook for 40 minutes.

Egg
Mayonnaise
(page 19)

Baked Quails' Egg
(page 20)
with Mustard
Dressing
(page 21)

Coddled
Egg
(page 20)

CHICKEN BROTH WITH PRUNES AND BACON

I got my friendly Old English sheepdog – Ozzie – nearly ten years ago after she had been rescued from being chained up in a deserted garage in Oswaldthwistle. She had a dislocated jaw, two broken paws, had to have fifty odd stitches, and was in the animal hospital for six weeks. When she came home it was bedlam initially: within the space of minutes she was alternately timid, nervous, bouncy, bewildered, lovable and then completely withdrawn. The first meal she had (the remnants of a leg of lamb), she devoured at a swifter speed than any hoover could clear a mess, but within minutes everything was brought back on the carpet. She became terribly frightened as if she would get another beating for doing something wrong.

It took several days to discover that what was best for her was simple roast chicken: not a recipe that has appeared in any book of mine, but simply put in the oven with a little salt and the merest smear of olive oil and then roasted for 1½ hours. This relatively expensive chore is repeated each Monday, Wednesday and Friday, but the carcasses provide me with a source of super stock at the farm. Take off all the white meat left on the carcass – you'll be surprised at how much you can get – and keep it for the broth. Make stock from the bones in your usual way. If you haven't time, use bought chicken stock from the supermarket.

This broth is quite filling and substantial, and fairly rich. It can be gilded by a generous slurp of sherry poured into each bowl at the very end.

---

12 dried prunes

10 fl oz (300 ml) cider of choice

2 tablespoons garlic or other oil of choice

6 oz (175 g) smoked bacon, finely diced

1 lb (450 g) root vegetables of choice, peeled and finely diced (parsnips, carrots, turnips, swedes, celeriac, etc.)

8 oz (225 g) cooked chicken, finely cut

1½ pints (900 ml) good chicken stock (see left)

2 tablespoons finely chopped parsley

Simmer the prunes in the cider for about 12 minutes then strain, retaining the cider. Remove the flesh from the prunes, and chop into large even pieces. Throw the stones away.

In a large frying pan heat the oil and cook the smoked bacon, stirring every 2–3 minutes, for about 12 minutes. Using a slotted spoon, remove on to a double thickness of kitchen paper to drain.

Brown the diced vegetables in the same oil and the bacon fat. This will take about 10 minutes. Drain well. All this preparation can be done in advance.

When ready to serve, pre-heat the oven to 200°C/400°F/Gas 6.

Divide the smoked bacon, prune and chicken flesh between four soup bowls.

Heat in the pre-heated oven for 10 minutes. Put the vegetables, chicken stock and retained cider into a large saucepan and reheat for just over 5 minutes.

Divide the soup and vegetables between the bowls and serve garnished with chopped parsley.

EGG MAYONNAISE

This is nursery food at its best but so often, when served up in restaurants, it is dull, dull, dull, nigh boring.

I am fortunate as I get most of my eggs from a smallholding in the Winster Valley; they have lovely, rich, deep orange yolks, and are full of flavour.

8 large eggs

16 thin asparagus spears, trimmed (see page 54)

salt

4 oz (100 g) lettuce, finely shredded

a good 10 fl oz (300 ml) Quick Mayonnaise (see page 21)

16 anchovies

64 small capers, drained

paprika

I normally boil my eggs in my chip pan and basket (devoid of fat, naturally). I can lower all eight eggs in the basket into the boiling water at the same time. When it comes back to boiling, I cook the eggs for *exactly* 4 minutes, and then take the chip container out and plunge it with the eggs immediately into a sink of very, very cold water. I leave it there until the eggs are quite cold.

Cook the asparagus lightly in boiling salted water. Drain and leave to cool. (Or you can cook them as in the recipe on page 54.)

Have your lettuce leaves divided between the plates. Shell the eggs then take one at a time to one plate and cut down the middle lengthwise. The yolks will be slightly soft, but this adds to the nursery-like texture. Place four halves, yolk side down, on each plate and then in between them put four thin asparagus spears. Put a dessertspoon of mayonnaise over each egg half and then on top of each dressed egg put a strip of anchovy that has been cut in half, forming a cross. In each part of the cross put a small caper (all in all you will need 64 capers). Put a pinch of paprika on each egg half and serve immediately with buttered slices of brown bread or, better still, the hot Savoury Dinner Rolls on page 66.

CODDLED EGGS

Years ago I was given four beautiful coddled egg 'cups' with 'silver' screw-tops, and I've had them on display on the kitchen dresser ever since. Recently, however, I had an invalid staying with me, during which time I rediscovered the joys of coddling eggs. Most coddlers will only take small eggs, which are even better for a person simply needing a very light course.

Pre-heat the oven to 180°C/350°F/Gas 4.

In the base of each container put a teaspoon of cooked chopped mushrooms, then break the small egg in on top. Season with salt and freshly ground black pepper, and then top with a ½ teaspoon of *fromage frais*. Bake in a bain-marie filled with hot water in the pre-heated oven for 10 minutes.

The teaspoon of mushroom can, if you wish, be substituted with virtually anything: leftover flaked fish; diced chicken or turkey; smoked salmon ends. Serve with soldiers of warm unbuttered toast as they can then be used to dunk and to soak the yolk and cream up.

BAKED QUAILS' EGGS

Easily obtained nowadays from supermarkets and good fishmongers' shops, these wonderful little items not only look appetising, but are very tasty used in many cold dishes such as Prawn Cocktail, Egg Mayonnaise and My Salade Niçoise (see pages 26, 19 and 70).

I use my mini mince pie tins for this – they're no bigger than an inch (2.5 cm) in diameter – and in the base of each I put less than ½ teaspoon of oil (as usual, of your own choice). Using a small serrated knife, it is an easy task to crack open each quail egg and turn it out into each circular indentation in the tin. In the oven pre-heated to 180°C/350°F/Gas 4, they take only 4 minutes to cook. Turn them out using the handle end of a teaspoon.

QUICK MAYONNAISE

For more years than I care to remember I have made mayonnaise using egg yolks only and an electric hand-beater. I used to kid myself that the time spent was therapeutic and that it was the only real way to make the stuff. Now that I'm in my sixties, I realise that speed is of the essence in the kitchen, although not at the expense of standards.

I invariably double up on the following recipe as it stores well in a screw-top jar in the fridge. You could use 5 fl oz (150 ml) each of oil and dry white wine instead of just the oil. The dressing will be less oily in texture, and will also be runnier.

2 medium eggs

½ teaspoon salt

½ teaspoon caster sugar

½ teaspoon dry English mustard powder

2 teaspoons fresh lemon juice

1 tablespoon white wine vinegar

10 fl oz (300 ml) good quality olive oil of choice

Put everything except the oil into your food processor and whizz round to blend. Dribble the oil in quite slowly with the machine turning. It's very quickly made.

GARLIC MAYONNAISE

Add 3 skinned and crushed fresh garlic cloves, or 2 heaped teaspoons of a good garlic paste (see page 8).

MUSTARD DRESSING

Add a further 1 tablespoon dry English mustard powder.

GARLIC TOMATO DRESSING

Add 1 teaspoon garlic paste and 2 teaspoons tomato paste to the mustard dressing. (You could also add 1 teaspoon horseradish cream – experiment!)

PEPPER AND ONION CASSEROLE WITH BAKED EGG

In the early years at Miller Howe when both staff and guests were in short supply, Sunday was the day each and every week that the whole of the kitchen was topped and tailed. Ovens were moved away from the walls and cleaned from top to bottom; hot cupboards were emptied and scrubbed out; walls were washed down; machines were polished, and drawers and shelves tidied. With so much time spent on these chores, this dish – which is so simple to put together – invariably started the evening meal. We called it *chachouka* then, and this recipe following is my new 1990s version.

garlic paste

2 oz (50 g) butter

8 oz (225 g) onions, peeled and thinly sliced

8 oz (225 g) red peppers, seeded and thinly sliced

4 medium eggs

freshly ground black pepper

Rub garlic paste round the inside of four size 5 Apilco dishes. Use a little or a lot, according to personal taste.

Melt the butter in a medium frying-pan and fry the onion and pepper gently for 6–10 minutes until soft and golden. Then transfer to the four prepared dishes and leave, covered with cling film, for up to a day.

When you wish to cook, pre-heat the oven to 180°C/350°F/Gas 4.

Make a well in the middle of the onion and pepper into which you break an egg. Bake in the pre-heated oven for 8–10 minutes until the yolk is soft and the white slightly opaque. Serve at once topped with lots of freshly ground black pepper.

DRESSED SPINACH WITH SCRAMBLED EGGS, SMOKED BACON AND GARLIC CROUTONS

Fresh spinach is always eagerly awaited from the lovely folk who have a small-holding at Winster near to the hotel. We seem to be well supplied from the end of July until early November.

In this recipe the shredded spinach is served raw, but I must also say that it can be fried in a deep-fryer at 180°C/350°F which takes about 3 minutes, and is an interesting variation on this dish.

6 oz (175 g) spinach, weighed after removing the tough stalks

1 tablespoon garlic oil

4 oz (100 g) smoked bacon, rinded and finely diced

2 slices bread, crusts removed, cut into small croûtons

SCRAMBLED EGGS

2 teaspoons olive oil

2 oz (50 g) butter, melted

4 medium eggs, lightly beaten

Prepare and wash the spinach and then dry it thoroughly in a salad drier. Roll about six to eight leaves up into the shape of a thick cigar and lie each cigar down on your work surface. Slice it very thinly indeed. Divide between four plates.

Heat the garlic oil in a small frying-pan and fry off the diced bacon until nice and crisp. Remove with a slotted spoon and keep warm. Fry the croûtons until crisp in the oil and bacon fat remaining in the pan. This usually takes about 4–5 minutes. Drain on kitchen paper.

For the scrambled eggs, melt the oil and butter together in a clean saucepan. Into this pour the beaten eggs. Cook until soft and runny, then spoon on to the spinach. Scatter with the croûtons and bacon, and serve.

DEEP-FRIED SAVOY CABBAGE WITH BUTTERED EGGS

This is a last-minute dish, but the texture and flavours are wonderful.

8 oz (225 g) green Savoy cabbage, finely shredded (as above)

oil for deep-frying

2 tablespoons sesame seeds, toasted (see page 55)

BUTTERED EGGS

6 medium eggs

salt and freshly ground black pepper

3 oz (75 g) butter

3 tablespoons crème fraîche

TO SERVE

16 fresh chives

36 small capers

Heat your deep-fryer to 180°C/350°F and cook the prepared cabbage in a large metal sieve in batches for just 1 minute until the edges start to go brown. Remove and turn on to a double thickness of kitchen paper. (I use a sieve rather than the usual fryer container.)

Meanwhile, break the eggs into a mixing bowl and season. Using a wire whisk, lightly beat together. Melt the butter over a medium heat in a saucepan. When it starts to bubble, add the eggs, and continue to whisk for about 3 minutes until the eggs begin to thicken. Remove from the heat and beat in the *crème fraîche*. Should it be too runny for your liking, put back on the hob for a minute, but stir all the time.

Divide the cooked cabbage into four portions, making nests on your individual plates, and scatter with the sesame seeds. Portion your cooked eggs into the middle. Then decorate with four chives to make a noughts-and-crosses board, putting a caper in each square. Serve at once.

Pepper and
Onion
Casserole
with
Baked Egg
(page 22)

Dressed Spinach with
Scrambled Eggs,
Smoked Bacon
and
Garlic Croûtons
(page 22)

Deep-fried
Savoy
Cabbage
with
Buttered Eggs
(page 23)

PRAWN COCKTAIL

I always remember, when working years ago in the banqueting kitchens of the Pierre Hotel in New York, seeing the afternoon staff coming on at three. They started preparing prawn cocktails for the evening service, wheeling out four enormous shelved trolleys lined with Manhattan glasses. Endless trays were brought out and shreds of iceberg lettuce plonked in the base of the glasses. Frozen prawns – and I *mean* frozen – were then taken handful by handful and tightly squeezed to make them go soft before putting them on top of the lettuce. The finishing touch was a spoonful of a commercial Marie Rose sauce. Needless to say, later that night, practically every single prawn cocktail came back, having just been played with by the no doubt horrified diners.

10 oz (300 g) frozen prawns, defrosted (see page 7)

20 baby asparagus spears, weighing about 3 oz (75 g), trimmed (see page 54)

4 tablespoons oil of choice

1 dessertspoon balsamic vinegar

4 oz (100 g) smoked salmon, cut into 16 thin slivers

2 oz (50 g) iceberg lettuce, very thinly sliced

4 sun-dried tomatoes, finely chopped

4 tablespoons Garlic Tomato Dressing (see page 21)

4 cherry tomatoes, cut into quarters

4 sprigs fresh parsley

Make sure the prawns are thoroughly defrosted. Dry them well.

Cook the asparagus in the hot oil for 4 minutes then, still on the heat, add the balsamic vinegar. Remove immediately from the heat and leave to cool.

Put four thin slivers of smoked salmon at even intervals around the insides of each Manhattan glass. Place in between four asparagus spears, tips to the top. Into the base of each glass tuck the shredded lettuce and on top of this the sun-dried tomatoes. Add the prawns, and coat with the dressing. Garnish with four quarters of cherry tomato, finishing each glass off with the last asparagus spear and a sprig of parsley.

A quarter of lemon part cut through base of flesh and skin would certainly be the cherry on the cake as far as garnishing goes.

CHILLED CONSOMME PRAWNS WITH SUN-DRIED TOMATOES AND CREME FRAICHE

This is a sort of cowboy prawn cocktail, and is very much a store-cupboard dish, but it's very delicious and very quick to prepare. You could make it with *crème fraîche* or soured cream, and you can even make the latter at home if you haven't got any around. It only takes about 30 minutes to sour 10 fl oz (300 ml) double cream by lightly beating in the juice of a ½ lemon.

The dish looks best if you use Manhattan cocktail glasses. These are relatively inexpensive (go to your nearest IKEA or Reject China Shop where they are around the pound mark), and are most useful for lots of puddings as well.

1 x 10 oz (295 g) tin condensed beef consommé, chilled

about 2 oz (50 g) iceberg lettuce, finely sliced

8 oz (225 g) frozen prawns, defrosted (see page 7)

4 tablespoons crème fraîche (or soured cream)

2 oz (50 g) sun-dried tomatoes, finely chopped

Line the base of each Manhattan glass with some of the roughly set beef consommé. Or you could set it from liquid in the base of the glasses for a smoother effect. Top with the shredded lettuce, then with the prawns, *crème fraîche* and tomato. What could be simpler!

POTTED PRAWNS IN SMOKED SALMON

I have always been a lover of potted Morecambe Bay shrimps but, knowing what is poured into this estuary these days, I am somewhat put off. When I served this dish for the first time to my lovely friends who take over the farm each January when they look after Ozzie, their faces were a picture. In answer to my question, 'What's wrong?', they said that it looked very rich. It *does* look rich, I agree, but it isn't to the palate, provided you let it come round to room temperature before serving.

a little butter for greasing the ramekins

4 oz (100 g) smoked salmon, in thin slices

6 oz (175 g) frozen prawns, defrosted (see page 7)

2 oz (50 g) butter, melted and cooled

2 heaped tablespoons crème fraîche

4 teaspoons Pernod

2 teaspoons horseradish cream

½ nutmeg, freshly grated

TO SERVE

about 2 oz (50 g) lettuce, shredded

2 teaspoons Vinaigrette (see page 83)

Grease four 3 in (7.5 cm) ramekins with a little butter, then line with the thinly sliced smoked salmon. If your slices of salmon are wide, make sure the overlap is at the *top* of the dish. Mix the other ingredients together gently and divide between the four dishes. Flip any excess smoked salmon over the top, then chill.

To serve, bring out of the fridge and leave to come round to room temperature, about 30 minutes. Lightly stroke a knife between smoked salmon and edge of ramekin, and turn each portion out on to individual plates, decorated with dressed lettuce.

Prawn
Cocktail
(page 26)

Potted
Prawns in
Smoked
Salmon
(page 27)

Chilled Consommé
Prawns with
Sun-dried Tomatoes and
Crème Fraîche
(page 26)

FRIED CHICKEN LIVERS

Chicken livers are an important and nutritious food, but I have discovered that people either love or loathe them. I feel sorry for the latter, as they are missing out on a relatively cheap and extremely versatile food.

Once you have mastered the very simple cooking technique below, there are a huge number of ways in which you can vary the dish. After 2 minutes' cooking time you can pour in a tablespoon of sherry, port, Marsala (my favourite), Madeira or a cheap cooking brandy. If you are using a gas hob you could well flambé this to add a bit of showmanship to the occasion (but difficult to do on the modern flat-topped electric hobs). A heaped tablespoon of finely chopped parsley divided between the four dishes not only adds colour but more taste. Even better than this is a level tablespoon of chopped parsley plus a level tablespoon of chopped marjoram. I also occasionally put four dried leaves of sage in with the chicken livers when I put them into the hot oil and remove prior to serving. I like the livers served with some deep-fried celeriac 'spaghetti' (see page 142).

12 oz (350 g) chicken livers

10 fl oz (300 ml) cold milk

2 tablespoons oil of choice

Try and buy the livers fresh rather than frozen, they're much nicer. Small tapestry scissors are useful for cutting away any signs of yellow or orange around, or any bits of gristle. Soak the cleaned livers in the cold milk, covered, in the fridge for at least 4 hours. Drain the livers and pat dry on kitchen paper. (The milk could be used in a sauce or soup, but I find that my next-door neighbours' cats love it!)

In a small frying pan of about 10 in (25 cm) in diameter, heat the oil through for about 5 minutes. (If you are lucky enough to encounter pirri-pirri oil, a chilli oil, do try it.) Toss the chicken livers in the bubbling oil for 3 minutes, stirring all the time. Remove with a slotted spoon and serve more or less immediately, on 2–3 oz (50–75 g) tagliatelli per person, or on Garlic Puréed Potatoes (see page 139).

If you are a greedy pig like me, have a slice of bread to hand for yourself, and as you take the cooked livers out of the frying pan mop up the bits and eat the sloppy slice quickly!

CHICKEN LIVER PARFAIT

If these are cooked in ramekins lined with cling film, the end result looks quite stunning. There is a rippled effect on the top, and the marbled look of the liver and cream sides is a joy. The parfaits can be made the evening before and chilled; you must bring them to room temperature before serving.

oil for greasing the ramekins

8 oz (225 g) chicken livers, trimmed and soaked overnight in milk to cover

5 fl oz (150 ml) double cream

1 medium egg

1 teaspoon Bovril

1 teaspoon garlic paste

a pinch of freshly grated nutmeg

1 tablespoon port

TO SERVE

chilled tinned beef consommé or a tomato and basil salad

Lightly grease four 3 in (7.5 cm) ramekins, and then line with cling film, making sure you stick it firmly to the bottom and sides. Pre-heat the oven to 160°C/325°F/Gas 3.

Strain the livers, then put with all the remaining ingredients into your food processor, and whizz around for a couple of minutes. Strain into a pouring jug and then divide between the four ramekins. Put the dishes into a small roasting tray and pour in enough boiling water to come half-way up the dishes. Bake in the pre-heated oven for 20 minutes, then remove from the oven and tray and leave to go cold.

Turn out, using the cling film to do so, and serve surrounded with some chilled beef consommé or with a tomato and basil salad.

Black Pudding
with
Diced Leeks
on a Baked
Apple Circle
(page 34)

Fried
Chicken
Livers
(page 30)
with
tagliatelle

Chicken Liver Parfait
(page 31)
with a tomato and
basil salad and
chilled beef
consommé

BLACK PUDDING WITH DICED LEEKS ON A BAKED APPLE CIRCLE

It is always a joy for me to visit Bury open market on a Saturday when it is a hive of activity. As the afternoon draws on, there are some mind-boggling 'bargains' to be had as fresh products are reduced in price. Some of the frozen gâteaux and turkey legs which have obviously been out on show for some time go for literally peanuts; the flower stalls want to get rid of everything; and bakers virtually give their remaining cobs, baps and buns away. But the black pudding stall keeps on churning out its various items at a rate of knots, and with no price reduction. They can be bought cold for cooking at home, but many locals buy their favourite kind served hot wrapped in greaseproof paper, and eat it there and then whilst wandering up and down the jam-packed aisles.

Black puddings have hit some of the newer London restaurants of late, and have even become fashionable. We recently cooked dinners in Johannesburg and Cape Town, and the main course was beef olives, one filled with a black pudding stuffing, which caused a great stir (see page 109).

butter

6 oz (175 g) good black pudding, skinned and cut into thin circles

1 English eating apple, cored (but not peeled), cut into four rings

6 oz (175 g) leeks, finely diced, washed and dried

Pre-heat the oven to 180°C/350°F/Gas 4, and lightly butter a baking tray.

Place the black pudding rounds on to the baking tray, making them into four circles. These should be the size of the apple rings; lay one down, then another half on top, going round to make a circle. Put the apple rings alongside, on the same tray. Bake in the pre-heated oven for 7 minutes only.

Meanwhile, fry the leeks in 2 oz (50 g) of the butter for about 4 minutes.

Transfer the apple slices to individual heated plates. Using a fish slice, put the circles of black pudding on top, and then scatter with the cooked leek. A spoonful of *fromage frais* on top of each tasty circle makes this a dish fit for a king.

AUBERGINE GALETTE

Prepare the aubergine slices and basic filling well in advance, then fry and fill at the last moment so the aubergine slices remain crisp.

1–2 aubergines, weighing about 1¼ lb (550 g) in total when peeled

salt and freshly ground black pepper

3 oz (75 g) Parmesan cheese, finely grated

1 teaspoon each of Worcestershire sauce and English mustard powder

2 teaspoons horseradish cream

½ teaspoon walnut oil

4 oz (100 g) plain flour

6 tablespoons oil of choice

TO SERVE

Tomato Sauce (see page 39)

Cut twelve very thin rounds of aubergine, weighing altogether about 4 oz (100 g). Lay on a cooling rack over kitchen paper, lightly salt, and leave for at least 4 hours. Using the rest of the aubergine, finely dice it, then steam over boiling water for 5 minutes. Put into a food processor and process until you get a mince-like texture. Put into a plastic sieve and leave for at least 4 hours to drain. This can all be done the day before.

Put the minced aubergine back into the food processor and process with the Parmesan, Worcestershire sauce, mustard, horseradish and walnut oil until a smooth paste is formed. Warm this through gently in a small pan while you fry the aubergine slices.

Season the flour and use it to coat each of the twelve aubergine slices. Fry in the very hot oil for at least 5 minutes, or until very crisp and nicely browned. Remove to kitchen paper and drain well.

Place a hot round of the fried aubergine on each plate and cover these with half the warmed puréed mix. Add a further aubergine round, the balance of the aubergine purée, and top with the third aubergine round. Serve immediately with warm Tomato Sauce (see page 39).

Aubergine
Goat Cheese
Custard
(page 38)
with Tomato Sauce
(page 39)

Aubergine
Galette
(page 35)
on
Tomato Sauce
(page 39)

AUBERGINE GOAT CHEESE CUSTARD

During a recent demonstration on a day course at the farm, one participant reacted to this dish with horror, as, apparently, even the thought of goat cheese made her bilious. Can't think why. She asked me for a substitute and, for once, I was lost for words.

We featured this recipe when working in South Africa earlier this year, but we cooked the filling in pastry cases using muffin tins (see page 71) instead of ramekins. We also added a hint of ground cumin to the dish, and it was an ideal accompaniment to the main course of Savoury Beef Olives (see page 109). It's a good starter as well, and although it can't really be prepared too much in advance, it's very easy and delicious when fresh.

8 thin slices of aubergine, peeled

salt

a little butter for greasing the ramekins

4 oz (100 g) onions, peeled and finely chopped

4 oz (100 g) red peppers, seeded and finely chopped

2 tablespoons olive oil

4 x ¼ in (5 mm) circles of your favourite goat cheese

5 fl oz (150 ml) double cream

1 medium egg

1 medium egg yolk

½ nutmeg, freshly grated

TO SERVE

Tomato Sauce (see opposite)

Cut the aubergine slices to fit the diameter of your ramekins *less* ⅛ in (3 mm). I use 3 in (7.5 cm) ramekins. Sprinkle the aubergine slices with salt and leave to drain on a cooling rack over kitchen paper (to catch the juices) for at least an hour. You'll be amazed at the amount of liquid that comes out. Pat dry.

Pre-heat the oven to 190°C/375°F/ Gas 5. Lightly butter the insides of your four ramekins.

Fry the onion and red pepper in the oil until golden, then leave to cool.

Place one circle of aubergine in each ramekin and on top of this put an eighth of the cooked onion and red pepper mix. On top of this put the cheese circles, followed by another eighth of the onion and red pepper mix, finishing off with the final aubergine slice.

Lightly beat the cream, eggs and nutmeg together and divide between the four ramekins, allowing the custard to sink down and between the layers.

Place your ramekins in a small roasting tray and pour in enough boiling water to come half-way up their sides. Place carefully in the pre-heated oven and cook for 30 minutes.

Leave for 10 minutes to cool, and then run a small sharp knife round the edges. Turn out on to individual plates, and serve with warm Tomato Sauce.

TOMATO SAUCE

I used to make very complicated tomato sauces, stewing fresh tomatoes with onion, garlic, sherry, chicken stock and basil very gently for up to an hour to allow them to reduce to the right consistency. I have since discovered that some supermarkets sell chopped tomatoes with basil in tins, and these take much less time to reduce to the correct texture, vital when you're entertaining and you don't have much time. I hardly miss the other flavourings – in fact the sauce often tastes much fresher.

2 x 14 oz (397 g) tins chopped tomatoes with basil

salt and freshly ground black pepper

Put the tomatoes and their juices into a suitable pan and simmer over a very low heat, uncovered, to reduce, stirring every now and again, until the tomatoes become a thick paste. This will take about 15 minutes. Season to taste.

If you like your sauce to be smooth, pass it through a coarse sieve; otherwise it's perfectly fine as it is for most purposes. It's best eaten as soon as possible, but you can store it in the fridge for a day or so.

Salami
Rounds
(page 42)
with
Pesto Sauce
(page 55)

Home-made
Apple
Chutney
(page 42)

Pasta
with
Sherried
Dried
Mushrooms
(page 43)

SALAMI ROUNDS

I have always loved the various Italian and Spanish *salami* in the past, shaving the slices wafer thin and using them as part of an hors d'oeuvre dish, but I now serve the following supper dish for friends. Accompanied by the Garlic Puréed Potatoes on page 139, it could actually be the main part of your meal.

Get four different *salami* from your delicatessen, preferably the same size in diameter as the crusty white baton loaves that many supermarkets now bake on their premises. You need one of those as well.

Ask for four thickish rounds of each salame to be sliced on their machine. Cut sixteen circles from the white baton: on each of eight of these put a teaspoon of red wine; on each of the other eight of these put a teaspoon of garlic oil.

Get your grill really, really hot, and bring salted water in the bottom of a steamer to boiling point.

Lay the salami slices in your steamer tray, cover with the lid, and steam for 5 minutes. Toast the bread slices on each side for 1 minute under the very hot grill. Put the four types of salami slices on the hot toast rounds and serve at once.

Garlic or other mayonnaise or dressing is good as an accompaniment, and so is a teaspoon of Apple Chutney (following) or Pesto Sauce (see page 55).

HOME-MADE APPLE CHUTNEY

Chutneys are quite cheap to make at home, take little or no time to prepare and cook, and are so much better than the run-of-the-mill commercial stuff. In the old days, each season had its relevant produce for making cheap chutneys, but nowadays, with most vegetables and fruits available throughout the year, a chutney can be made just when it takes your fancy!

This apple chutney is relatively sweet, and is ideal on a ploughman's platter, especially if you serve the potato bread on page 66 with it. I also find myself using a dessertspoon of it, lightly heated through, with baked chicken drumsticks, lamb chops and rump steaks, both grilled.

8 oz (225 g) onions, peeled and finely chopped

1½ lb (675 g) cooking apples, peeled, cored and roughly chopped

1 pint (600 ml) malt vinegar

12 oz (350 g) soft brown sugar

4 oz (100 g) sultanas

½ oz (15 g) mixed spice

½ oz (15 g) coarse sea salt

Put the onion into a pan of lightly salted boiling water, bring back to the boil and cook for 5 minutes. Drain the onion and wipe the pan dry.

Put all the remaining ingredients, including the onion, into the pan and simmer over a low heat for 1½ hours until thick and dry. Stir from time to time with a wooden spoon. The chutney is ready when a spoon quickly 'swept' through the base of the pan leaves no signs of liquid.

Meanwhile, wash and sterilise two 1 lb (450 g) jars. Wash with boiling water, then dry and put in a warm oven for 30 minutes. While warm, fill with the chutney, then cool. When cold, cover with cling film and then the screw-tops if relevant. Use up within three months.

PASTA WITH SHERRIED DRIED MUSHROOMS

This is a very rich dish, one which I first served one night after giving a food and flower demonstration. The car broke down on the way home, so the restaurant where we should have had dinner was well and truly closed when we passed by. Always having dried pasta and packets of dried *porcini* or ceps in the store-cupboard, the dish turned out to be quite a success, and the washed-out evening became an occasion!

Pasta packets always claim that 4 oz (100 g) is a normal portion per person. Normal for whom – Gulliver? I find 3 oz (75 g) generous, and 2 oz (50 g) sufficient. Use however much pasta *you* like, but the following is sufficient for four.

4 oz (100 g) dried porcini (ceps)

10 fl oz (300 ml) sherry of choice

4 tablespoons double cream

8 oz (225 g) pasta (tagliatelli are good)

4 oz (100 g) Parmesan cheese, freshly grated

4 tablespoons freshly chopped parsley

Soak the dried mushrooms in the sherry for about 30 minutes. Strain the mushrooms and leave to one side, retaining the sherry. In a small saucepan, reduce the sherry by half, about 5 minutes. Stir in the double cream, cook for another minute, then add the mushrooms and cook for a further minute.

In the meantime, cook the pasta according to the directions on the packet. Strain, put on to your warmed plates and divide the mushrooms between the four. Pass the Parmesan and parsley around separately.

Cream
Sauce
(page 47)

Savoury Mushrooms
with
Bolognese,
Boursin
and Spinach
(page 46)

Mushroom
Caps in
Garlic
Cream
Sauce
(page 47)

Irish
Farm
Mushroom
Roquefort
'Baps'
(page 46)

IRISH FARM MUSHROOM ROQUEFORT 'BAPS'

Large field mushrooms are ideal for this, but stick to the cultivated ones available from the supermarket.

8 large Irish farm mushrooms, about 2 oz (50 g) each when skinned and stalked

8 dessertspoons melted butter

4 slices good smoked bacon, weighing at least 1 oz (25 g) each, rinded

6 oz (175 g) Roquefort cheese

Pre-heat the oven to 180°C/350°F/Gas 4.

Place all the prepared mushroom caps, brown inner side up, on a baking tray, and on to each put a dessertspoon of melted butter. On the same tray put the bacon slices, then bake in the pre-heated oven for 5 minutes. (Strain any excess butter off into your butter pan, and reserve for another use.)

In a bowl lightly cream the soft Roquefort cheese. Divide between four of the mushroom caps, putting the other mushroom caps on top to make 'burger baps'. Loosely drape over each the partly cooked bacon. They can now be left for at least a few hours.

When you wish to serve, the oven should be pre-heated again, but to 200°C/400°F/Gas 6. The mushrooms take only 8 minutes to warm through, melting the cheese.

SAVOURY MUSHROOMS WITH BOLOGNESE, BOURSIN AND SPINACH

Simple and very delicious. The combination of My Bolognese and Boursin is a successful one, and I use it elsewhere as a pancake filling (see page 74).

oil for greasing the dishes

4 oz (100 g) frozen chopped leaf spinach, defrosted

4 dessertspoons crème fraîche

freshly ground black pepper

8 oz (225 g) button mushrooms (about 7 per portion)

8 oz (225 g) My Bolognese (see page 119)

8 oz (225 g) Boursin cream cheese

Oil four size 5 Apilco dishes. Spread a quarter of the chopped spinach on the base of each and put a dessertspoon of *crème fraîche* on top. Be very generous with the pepper. Arrange the mushrooms, hollow or stem end up, on top. Combine the Bolognese with the Boursin, and divide the mix between the mushroom bases. Leave until you are ready to cook.

When you wish to cook and serve, pre-heat the oven to 200°C/400°F/Gas 6. Bake the mushrooms for 10 minutes, and serve hot.

MUSHROOM CAPS IN GARLIC CREAM SAUCE

Try and use button mushrooms. If they are really small there is no need to remove the stalks. And if they look clean, for goodness' sake don't wash them, as this tends to affect both their texture and their taste.

a little butter for greasing the ramekins

6 oz (175 g) button mushroom caps

Garlic Cream Sauce (opposite)

1 tablespoon finely chopped parsley

Lightly butter four 3 in (7.5 cm) ramekins. Divide the mushroom caps between the buttered ramekins, and put in a roasting tray. Divide the Garlic Cream Sauce between the four ramekins. Pour enough boiling water into the roasting tray to come half-way up the sides of the ramekins, and cook on top of the stove for 12 minutes.

Serve the ramekins, on doyleyed plates, with a teaspoon and small fork. Sprinkle with the parsley.

CREAM SAUCE

This is a simple sauce, but it's delicious and very versatile. Basically it's reduced double cream with a flavouring added. For a cider cream sauce, one of my favourites, reduce 10 fl oz (300 ml) cider of choice to 2 tablespoons and add to the reduced cream. Do the same with Noilly Prat or white wine. For a brandy or Marsala cream sauce, reduce 5 fl oz (150 ml) liquor to 1 tablespoon and add to the reduced cream. For a garlic cream sauce, add 2 teaspoons garlic paste to the reduced cream.

1 pint (600 ml) double cream

a pinch of salt

flavouring of choice (see above)

Put the cream and salt into a fairly large saucepan. Place about a third of the pan's bottom only over the direct heat on the hob, because when the cream reaches the vital temperature, it has the unruly habit of coming suddenly to the boil and surging over the edge of the pan like the head of a badly served bottle of Guinness. Watch it like a hawk and, depending on the heat of the hob, your cream will be reduced by half in 15–20 minutes. Do not take it any further.

Add the flavouring chosen, and stir it in. Lo and behold, your sauce is made.

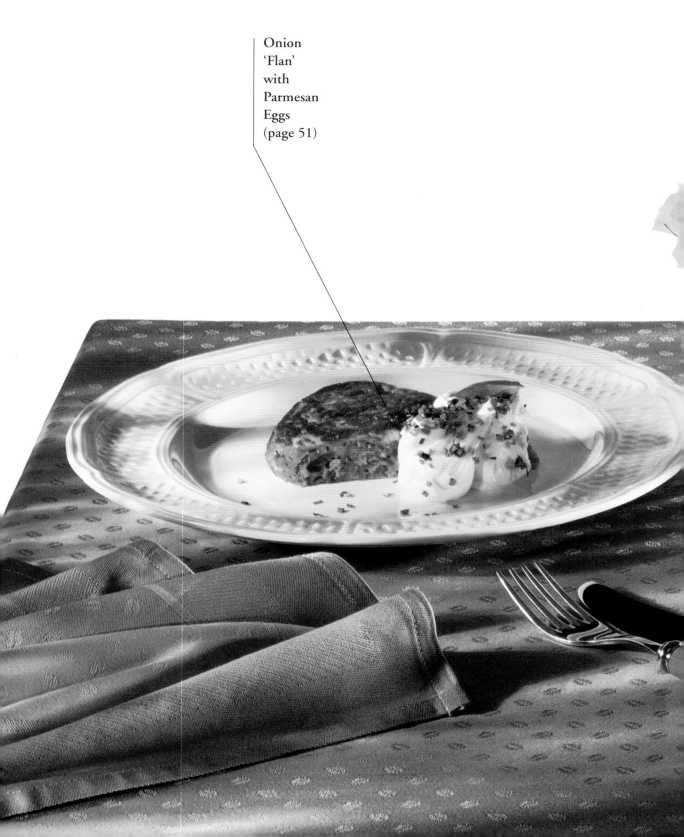

Onion
'Flan'
with
Parmesan
Eggs
(page 51)

Steamed Cauliflower
on
Tapenade
with
Hard-boiled Egg
(page 50)

STEAMED CAULIFLOWER ON TAPENADE WITH HARD-BOILED EGG

You must seek out a lovely fresh large cauliflower with little and clean outer stem leaves. The head should be creamy to white in complexion, and almost smiling at you: beware of loose heads and an oatmeal colour! Cook the cauliflower at the last minute, but most of the garnishes could have been prepared in advance.

1 x 1¾ lb (800 g) cauliflower

2 teaspoons salt

4 medium eggs

4 oz (100 g) flaked almonds, toasted (see page 179)

4 tablespoons Tapenade (right)

4 oz (100 g) mature Cheddar cheese, coarsely grated

Remove the thick stems and base of the root from the cauliflower. Plunge the head into a bowl of salted water and leave for 30 minutes. Then remove and drain.

Fill the base of a steamer saucepan with about 2 pints (1.2 litres) boiling water and add the salt. When it's back to the boil, put your cauliflower in, root side down, in the steamer part, place over the boiling water, and then cover firmly with the lid. The cauliflower will be cooked crisp in only 10 minutes, but if you like

yours falling apart (heaven forbid), give it 15 minutes.

In the meantime, hard-boil the eggs, then shell and pass through a fine plastic sieve. Have the toasted flaked almonds and the Tapenade to hand.

On each of your warm serving plates spread 1 tablespoon of the Tapenade, and on top of this place one-quarter wedge of the cauliflower. Scatter over each the sieved egg and flaked almonds. Pass the Cheddar around for each guest to help themselves.

TAPENADE

Make the tapenade – a deliciously flavoured purée of black olives from the south of France – the day before, and leave overnight in the fridge, covered with cling film. Keep any left over in the fridge: it's good on toast, or the croûtons on page 64, as a canapé.

25 stoned black olives

10 anchovy fillets

4 heaped tablespoons drained tinned tuna

2 tablespoons small drained capers

5 fl oz (150 ml) extra virgin olive oil

Put all the ingredients except for the oil in the food processor and begin to process at a high speed. Very slowly dribble in the oil, as if making a processor mayonnaise. When all the oil is in, the Tapenade is ready.

ONION 'FLAN' WITH PARMESAN EGGS

This is a cross between a flan and an omelette, and it's so tasty with the garlic and Parmesan.

12 oz (350 g) onions, peeled, quartered and thinly sliced

1 teaspoon garlic paste

2 tablespoons olive oil

2 tablespoons balsamic vinegar

2 tablespoons dry white wine

6 medium eggs

4 oz (100 g) Parmesan cheese, finely grated

2 tablespoons finely chopped parsley

TO SERVE

4 tablespoons fromage frais

1 small bunch chives, finely chopped

Fry the onion and garlic paste in the oil gently for 15 minutes, stirring from time to time with a wooden spoon. Add the vinegar and wine and fry for a further 5 minutes. At this stage you can leave the mixture to go cold, to be finished just prior to serving.

Beat together the eggs, Parmesan and parsley. Re-heat the onion mixture in an 8–10 in (20–25 cm) non-stick frying pan and pour on the egg mixture. Stir over a high heat for 5 minutes until the mixture begins to thicken. Bring it in continually from the sides, as you would an omelette.

When fairly well done on the base, put a dinner plate on top of the frying pan and turn the flan out on to it. Slide the other side back into the frying pan and cook for a further 5 or 6 minutes until you have a solid omelette.

Turn out and cut into four. Garnish each portion with a tablespoon of *fromage frais* and some finely chopped chives.

VARIATIONS

You can use 4 oz (100 g) each of coarsely grated carrot, apple and courgette instead of the onion, then mix in the eggs, cheese and parsley.

You can use 4 oz (100g) onion only, then add 4 oz (100 g) each of white crab-meat and defrosted prawns when you add the egg mixture. Use fresh dill instead of parsley.

Fried
Asparagus
with
Caper
Butter Sauce
(page 54)

Pesto
Sauce
(page 55)

Baked Mediterranean
Tomatoes with Pesto and
Bel Paese (page 55)

FRIED ASPARAGUS WITH CAPER BUTTER SAUCE

I always used to say that only Suffolk or Southport asparagus could be served during its short season. Now supermarkets have asparagus most weeks, and it is delicious. People often get bothered about just how much of the stem they should remove with their sharp knife. I don't use a knife. Simply take each spear in your hands and *bend*. It will naturally snap where the tender point starts and the tough bottom ends!

16 fresh asparagus spears, bottom stems removed (use in the stockpot), about 8 oz (225 g) in weight

2 tablespoons oil of choice

2 oz (50 g) butter

1 tablespoon balsamic vinegar

CAPER BUTTER SAUCE

4 oz (100 g) butter

2 tablespoons small capers, drained

Warm the oil in a suitable frying pan, add the butter and melt. Cook the asparagus for no more than 8 minutes, turning with a wooden spatula. Add the vinegar off the heat.

Meanwhile melt the butter for the sauce over high heat for 2 minutes, then add the capers. Heat through for a few seconds.

Divide the asparagus spears and their juices between four small plates and cover with the caper butter sauce. Serve immediately.

BAKED MEDITERRANEAN TOMATOES WITH PESTO AND BEL PAESE

This is simplicity itself. If you like, top with some chopped fresh chives and serve on a 3 in (7.5 cm) croûton (see page 64). This is more filling.

2 large tomatoes, weighing between 6 and 8 oz (175–225 g) each

4 teaspoons Pesto Sauce (right)

4 x 1 oz (25 g) individual Bel Paese cheeses

Wipe the tomatoes, then cut in half around the equators. Using a Parisian scoop, remove the hard stalk along with all the inner flesh and seeds, leaving a 'cup'. Into the middle of this put a teaspoon of pesto and then the Bel Paese. You can now leave it for up to a day, covered with cling film, in the fridge.

When you wish to serve, pre-heat the oven to 200°C/400°F/Gas 6. The tomato will be sufficiently cooked in 8 minutes.

PESTO SAUCE

My closest friends in the Cape have a lovely garden with *borders* of this delicious herb, basil, all in different colours – dark green, light green, slightly orange and deep red. The sauce that is made from basil, pesto, is very versatile, and I use it on pasta, on canapés, on fish, and with vegetables such as tomatoes.

In winter, when the basil we get is grown under cloches, it doesn't appear to have the same gutsy flavour as the leaves of the sunny summer plant, so increase the amount of leaves used to 3 oz (75 g).

1 heaped tablespoon pine kernels

2 oz (50 g) fresh basil leaves

1 teaspoon garlic paste

2 oz (50 g) Parmesan cheese, coarsely grated

2 teaspoons caster sugar

8 tablespoons olive oil

salt and freshly ground black pepper

First toast the pine kernels. Lay them flat on a baking tray and in a pre-heated oven at about 180°C/350°F/Gas 4 – preferably one you are using to cook something else – bake for about 12 minutes until they are lightly brown. (Use the same technique for other nuts and seeds, but watch carefully, they all brown at different rates, and dark brown nuts are *very* bitter.)

Blend all the ingredients together in a food processor, and store in a screw-top jar in the fridge.

Barbecued
Vegetables
with
Roquefort
and Pesto
(page 58)

Marinated
Peppers
(page 59)

Grilled Brie
with
Pernod
Figs and
Boursin
(page 58)

GRILLED BRIE WITH PERNOD FIGS AND BOURSIN

When buying Brie at the supermarket, it is often difficult to know if wedges or circles are ripe, because they are kept under refrigeration. The sell-by date is a very reliable source of information, but recently I bought a large round to finish off a dinner party and had I served it straight from the pack it would have finished off my reputation as it was so solid. Remembering a tip a friend in the Cape had given me, I found some thick brown paper which I put on the top of the cheese and with a medium-heat iron I caringly and coaxingly ironed away in a very gentle manner. In 2–3 minutes the Brie was creamy!

For four, the following recipe is gooey and different. Start the day before by marinating the figs, then grill and bring together at the last minute. It can also be served as a dessert-cum-cheese course.

8 fat dried figs

2 tablespoons Pernod

2 tablespoons water

4 teaspoons Boursin cream cheese

1 x 8 oz (225 g) wedge ripe Brie cheese

Marinate the dried figs in the Pernod and water for at least a day. They are then lovely and soft. Split in two and put a teaspoon of Boursin in each. Place on four individual plates.

Pre-heat the grill to its hottest.

Put the Brie on a small baking tray, and simply grill on both sides for about 2 minutes. Then cut into four smaller wedges and serve at once with the figs and Boursin.

BARBECUED VEGETABLES WITH ROQUEFORT AND PESTO

These vegetables are baked in the oven, but in the summer you could of course barbecue them briefly for that wonderful char-grill flavour.

1 red pepper, cut into quarters and fanned (see opposite)

1 fennel bulb, stalk removed, quartered

1 x 2 in (5 cm) middle section of aubergine, cut lengthways into 4 wedges

1 large courgette, topped and tailed, cut lengthways into 4 wedges

6 tablespoons balsamic vinegar

a little oil of choice for greasing

2 tablespoons Pesto Sauce (see page 55)

4 oz (100 g) Roquefort cheese, crumbled

Marinate the prepared vegetables in the balsamic vinegar overnight or for longer – up to a couple of days – then strain, retaining the vinegar.

Pre-heat the oven to 200°C/400°F/ Gas 6, and lightly oil a baking tray.

Pour the vinegar on to the baking tray and then build up four towers in the following order: fennel, aubergine, courgette, then red pepper. Bake in the pre-heated oven for 40 minutes.

Meanwhile pre-heat the grill to very hot.

Top each vegetable tower with a quarter of the pesto and the crumbled Roquefort, and grill until the cheese bubbles. Using a fish slice, transfer to warm plates, or you could serve the vegetable towers on the croûtons on page 64.

When the pepper strips are cold, season generously with black pepper and put into an airtight container. Cover with the dressing and leave for up to two days.

When you want to serve, put three different coloured halves on the dressed leaves on each plate, and sprinkle over the freshly chopped herbs.

MARINATED PEPPERS

Make sure when you buy the peppers that they are firm, brightly coloured with a glossy finish, and with no evidence of either brown or soft spots.

2 each of red, green and yellow peppers

salt and freshly ground black peppers

10 fl oz (300 ml) Vinaigrette (see page 83)

about 2 oz (50 g) assorted salad leaves, dressed

4 dessertspoons chopped fresh herbs

Cut the peppers in half lengthways and remove all the seeds. Take each pepper half, hold the stalk end in one hand and cut into strips about ¼ in (5 mm) apart, starting ½ in (1 cm) below the stalk, down through to the base. They are still held together at one end.

Steam over a pan of boiling seasoned water for 15 minutes.

clockwise on plate:
Bacon and Sun-dried Tomato Savoury Rounds
(topping 7, page 64)
Smoked Salmon and Cream Cheese Savoury Rounds
(topping 1, page 62)
Egg and Garlic Mayonnaise Savoury Rounds
(topping 6, page 63)

clockwise on plate:
Aubergine and Walnut Savoury Rounds
(topping 5, page 63)
Aubergine and Crème Fraîche Savoury
Rounds (topping 3, page 63)
Red Pepper and Bel Paese Savoury Rounds
(topping 4, page 63)
Chicken and Redcurrant Jelly Savoury
Rounds (topping 2, page 62)

SAVOURY ROUNDS

In my fridge, in empty sterilised screw-top honey jars, I always have at least three 'mixes' similar to those below. They are ideal for sandwiches for tea, or packed luncheons; some can be used to stuff chicken breasts that are to be baked (see page 99); others are delicious painted on to portions of marinated white fish to be baked or grilled.

But when I have friends round for supper, I offer them a plate of little savoury rounds as a canapé while I'm messing about in the kitchen. Basically savoury rounds are the croûtons mentioned on page 64, and they can be any size you like – canapé size or 3 in (7.5 cm) in diameter. Four of the latter, with different toppings, would also make a good starter.

The various mixtures are spooned or piped on the croûtons and then you can use your imagination and a little time tarting them up with little sprigs of fresh herbs, slices of stuffed olives, capers, circles of gherkins, redcurrants, toasted sesame seeds, poppy seeds or quarters of the lovely mini tomatoes now found in supermarkets. Do your Picasso bit and be proud of turning a little something into a great event.

The following small quantities can be whizzed up in a liquidiser but when doubled the texture is much smoother if done in a food processor. This latter way always means that the croûton toppings can be piped using a star nozzle, which makes them look even more professional. They can be prepared well in advance and chilled until you need to use them.

When making all the toppings, do please taste a fingertip-full, and you might find that a little more seasoning, a hint of a wine vinegar, a touch of creamed mustard or horseradish – or sometimes the merest hint of icing sugar – will bring the flavours together. At the end of the day it is what *you* like that you will serve to your family and friends.

TOPPING 1

6 oz (175 g) smoked salmon off-cuts

3 oz (75 g) cream cheese

1 level teaspoon caraway seeds

1 heaped teaspoon horseradish cream

3 generous sprigs fresh dill (if available)

Simply whizz everything together to a paste.

TOPPING 2

6 oz (175 g) cooked chicken bits

1 tablespoon Quick Mayonnaise (see page 21)

12 strips fresh chives

1 teaspoon redcurrant jelly

1 teaspoon made mustard

Simple whizz everything together to a paste.

TOPPING 3

8 oz (225 g) aubergine, sliced

salt

6 oz (175 g) onions, peeled and diced

1 tablespoon olive oil

2 oz (50 g) cream cheese

1 tablespoon crème fraîche

1 teaspoon tomato paste

1 teaspoon horseradish cream

Salt, drain and bake the aubergine slices as opposite. Fry the onion in the oil for about 8 minutes until soft. When cold, whizz to a paste with the remaining ingredients.

TOPPING 4

2 red peppers, seeded and cut into thin strips

a little olive oil

2 oz (50 g) Bel Paese cheese

1 dessertspoon balsamic vinegar

2 oz (50 g) macadamia nuts, toasted (see page 55)

Pre-heat the oven to 200°C/400°F/Gas 6.

Dribble the red pepper strips with a little oil, then bake in the pre-heated oven for 20 minutes. When cold, whizz to a paste with the remaining ingredients.

TOPPING 5

6 oz (175 g) aubergine, sliced

salt

4 oz (100 g) stoned olives

1 oz (25 g) shelled walnuts

½ teaspoon garlic paste

Pre-heat the oven to 200°C/400°F/Gas 6.

Sprinkle the aubergine slices with salt and leave on a rack over kitchen paper for at least 1 hour. Pat dry then bake in the pre-heated oven for 6 minutes. When cool, whizz to a paste with the remaining ingredients.

TOPPING 6

3 hard-boiled eggs, shelled when cold

1 heaped tablespoon Garlic Mayonnaise (see page 21)

1 tablespoon chopped parsley

3 gherkins

Simply whizz everything together to a paste.

TOPPING 7

6 oz (175 g) smoked bacon, diced

1 tablespoon garlic oil

2 oz (50 g) sun-dried tomatoes

4 fresh sage leaves

2 tablespoons oil of choice

2 oz (50 g) pine kernels, toasted (see page 55)

Cook the bacon in the garlic oil in a small frying pan for 10 minutes. When cold, whizz to a paste with the remaining ingredients.

SAVOURY CROUTONS

I am using croûtons more and more these days as they are simple, filling, relatively inexpensive and quite delicious. They can act as the base for so many things. When I demonstrate making them with butter, somebody always, inevitably, comes up with the query, 'Can you use margarine?' I have to be honest and say I never have. I don't like its flavour, and I've read that eating margarine actually is equivalent to painting your arteries with plastic! However, these days, with medical recommendations taking as many U-turns as the present Government, if one was to listen to everything they said one would be so confused that the mental hospitals would be even busier. Butter and good oils oil *my* working parts.

For small croûton dice, used for soups or salads, see the Dressed Spinach recipe on page 22. For garlic croûtons, you could infuse some crushed garlic in the butter while it is melting, before dipping the croûtons in it and baking.

4 x 3 in (7.5 cm) rounds of sliced bread, plus 2 oz (50 g) butter, melted

or

4 x 2 in (5 cm) rounds of sliced bread, plus 1 oz (25 g) butter, melted

Pre-heat the oven to 180°C/350°F/Gas 4.

Dip the bread rounds in the melted butter quickly – a kitchen fork is handy for this – and put on a baking tray. The larger rounds need only 15 minutes to bake through, and the smaller ones 10 minutes. Remove and put on a double thickness of kitchen paper to drain. Pour any surplus butter from the tray back into your butter saucepan and keep for another use.

CHOUX PASTRY CUPS

These little cups, made from choux pastry, are formed in six 3 in (7.5 cm) muffin tins (see page 71), and are very useful as a container for mixtures such as My Bolognese (see page 119), or some of the Savoury Round toppings on page 62, for instance. They can serve as canapés, as a starter with different fillings or as an accompaniment to meat, filled with something like Tapenade (see page 50) or a diced cooked vegetable, such as aubergine, red pepper, beetroot, carrot, celeriac, fennel, mushroom, or a mixture.

5 fl oz (150 ml) cold water

2 oz (50 g) butter, cut into very small pieces

2½ oz (65 g) strong plain flour

a generous pinch of salt

2 medium eggs, lightly beaten

Pre-heat the oven to 220°C/425°F/Gas 7. Rinse the muffin tins in cold water. Do not dry.

Place the water and butter in a saucepan and allow to melt over a very low heat. If the heat is high, the water will evaporate a little and won't be able to take up the flour. When melted, turn the heat up as high as possible and the mix will initially bubble and boil. At this stage, throw in the sifted flour and salt and, using a round-edged wooden spoon, bash the living daylights out of the mix, the back of the spoon beating against the sides of the saucepan. It is often easier to do this if you hold the spoon fairly low down the handle. The mixture looks rather unsightly.

Then, little by little, beat in your beaten egg. Do this slowly, taking some time, and never add and beat in more egg until the flour mixture has taken up the egg already in it. The initially dull basic roux will soon develop quite a sheen and a lovely texture. When it comes together in a ball and leaves the side of the pan clean, it is ready.

Put the dough into a piping bag and pipe a little into each damp muffin tin depression. With a wet thumb, work the mixture up the sides of the tins, to make a well defined nest or cup shape. Bake in the pre-heated oven for 10–15 minutes, until golden and crisp. You may need to scoop out some of the softer middle.

Leave to cool, or serve hot, depending on usage. Fill the cups at the last minute to avoid sogginess.

CHEESE, CHUTNEY, GARLIC AND POTATO BREAD

This is a delicious bread to have around for supper parties. It's great with soups, and magnificent with cheese. You may be a little alarmed at the thought of making bread in a hurry, but it really *is* very easy and quick, as it does not use yeast, so no rising and proving.

---

4 oz (100 g) Cheddar cheese, coarsely grated

---

1 heaped teaspoon garlic paste

---

12 oz (350 g) self-raising flour

---

12 oz (350 g) potatoes, peeled and coarsely grated

---

2 oz (50 g) sultanas

---

2 large tablespoons chutney of choice

---

2 oz (50 g) shelled mixed nuts, chopped

---

2 medium eggs, lightly beaten

---

5 oz (150 g) natural yoghurt

Pre-heat the oven to 180°C/350°F/Gas 4, and have ready a large baking tray lined with a double thickness of good grease-proof paper, sprinkled with plain flour.

Mix all the ingredients in a large mixing bowl. Tidy cooks then use a long-handled spoon to combine everything, but I use my hands! Spread the mixture on to the tray and pat it out to a circle with your hands. Using a palette knife, mark into twelve wedges, or less if wanted.

Bake in the oven for 1 hour. Eat warm.

SAVOURY DINNER ROLLS

Even if you're only serving a salad and some cheese, a simple supper will always look more impressive if you offer a home-made bread of some kind. These dinner rolls are wonderfully flavoured – with cheese, watercress and mustard – and they're not too difficult to make, even if they take a little time. They're best fresh, of course, but they could be made in advance then reheated gently.

MAKES 8–9 ROLLS

½ oz (15 g) fresh yeast

¼ teaspoon caster sugar

---

1 oz (25 g) butter, melted

---

8 oz (225 g) strong plain flour

---

1 oz (25 g) Cheddar cheese, finely grated

½ teaspoon salt

---

a few turns of freshly ground black pepper

½ bunch watercress, finely chopped

½ teaspoon dry English mustard powder

---

5 fl oz (150 ml) tepid milk

TO GARNISH

---

finely chopped nuts and/or cracked wheat

---

melted butter to paint

Cream the yeast with the caster sugar in a small basin using a wooden spoon and then combine with the cooled melted butter. Place the flour, cheese, salt, pepper, watercress and mustard in a food mixer bowl and fit on the dough hook. Add the tepid milk slowly to the yeast (the temperature should be like that of the water for a baby's bath: never, *ever* have it too hot or you will kill the yeast). With the machine on a slow speed, start to add the yeast and milk to the flour mixture. Carry on kneading slowly until the mixture is quite smooth and springy.

Take the dough out of the bowl and knead into a ball shape on a lightly floured surface. Lightly flour the mixer bowl as well, and return the ball of dough to it. Cover with a warm tea towel, and leave to prove in a warm draught-free corner of the kitchen. After 1 hour carefully look at the mixture and when it is literally doubled in size, knock back down with your fist, to more or less its original size. Turn out on to a floured board.

Cut the dough into eight or nine pieces to make individual rolls. To do this if right-handed, place your right-hand palm down on the board and then slowly bring your finger ends up underneath your palm. Put each individual piece of dough beneath this cup-shaped mitt, and roll your hand round in a circle, applying very little pressure, to make your cob rolls. Should your hands be hot and sweaty, lightly flour them.

Transfer the rolls to baking trays lined with greaseproof paper, allowing space round each for them to rise. At this stage you could sprinkle some finely chopped nuts and/or cracked wheat on top of each roll. Put the trays back into your warm spot and leave the rolls to double in size again, which normally takes about 30 minutes.

Meanwhile, pre-heat the oven to 230°C/450°F/Gas 8. Bake the rolls for 15–20 minutes. Remove from the oven, paint liberally with melted butter, and serve as soon as possible.

Cheese,
Chutney,
Garlic and
Potato
Bread
(page 66)

Savoury
Dinner
Rolls
(page 66)

Choux Pastry Cups
(page 65)
filled
with
My Bolognese
(page 119)

Choux Pastry Cups
(page 65)
filled
with
cheese and
herb pâté

Choux Pastry Cups
(page 65)
filled with
onion and
red pepper
casserole

My Salade Nicoise

Tinned tuna has long been a firm favourite of mine, and my store-cupboard is never without a half a dozen or so tins.

With all the bits and pieces in this platter, I find that you only need a very little tuna per person, so as well as being quick to do, it's very economical!

PER PERSON

2½ oz (65 g) tinned tuna, drained well

about ½ oz (15 g) iceberg lettuce, thinly sliced

2 sun-dried tomatoes, cut into thin strips

3 anchovies, cut in half and rolled into balls

4 capers

2 teaspoons freshly grated Parmesan cheese

1 teaspoon grated peeled onion

1 'soft' hard-boiled egg (see page 19), shelled and quartered, or 4 baked quails' eggs (see page 20)

4 fresh thin asparagus spears (never tinned), blanched

4 grapes, halved and pipped

1 tablespoon Garlic Tomato Dressing (see page 21)

Simply use a suitable plate and, starting with the lettuce, build everything decoratively up on top, finishing with the tuna flakes and the dressing. It is like an old-fashioned platter of hors d'oeuvres.

Yorkshire Pudding with Onion Gravy

This Yorkshire pudding mix, used as a delicious starter, will make four puddings using muffin tins of about 3 in (7.5 cm) in diameter and 1¾ in (4 cm) high. The Yorkshire puddings can be also used to accompany the roast beef on page 110.

3 oz (75 g) plain flour, sieved

1 medium egg

2½ fl oz (75 ml) cold water

2½ fl oz (75 ml) cold milk

salt and freshly ground black pepper

4 tablespoons beef dripping (or oil of choice)

ONION GRAVY

1½ lb (675 g) onions, peeled, quartered and cut into very thin slices

2 tablespoons olive oil

2 heaped teaspoons horseradish cream

7½ fl oz (225 ml) tinned condensed beef consommé

1 teaspoon Bovril

Put all the Yorkshire pudding ingredients, apart from the dripping, into a bowl and beat until you get a smooth batter. Cover with cling film and put in the fridge; this can be done in the morning.

When you wish to cook, pre-heat the oven to 220°C/425°F/Gas 7. Pre-heat a burner on the hob as well.

Put a tablespoon of beef dripping into each muffin tin and allow it to reach nigh boiling temperature in the oven (I give it a good 10 minutes). Bring the muffin tin tray out and place on the very hot hob, and divided the batter between the four tins. Return to the oven and they take 15–20 minutes to rise and become firm.

Meanwhile make the onion gravy. Fry the onion gently in the hot oil in a large pan for 12 minutes until soft. Add the remaining gravy ingredients and cook for a further 5 minutes.

When the Yorkshire puddings are cooked, simply cut a small hole out of each top, and divide the onion gravy between them. If you like, serve with the Buttered Caraway Cabbage on page 143, when it becomes a good main course.

MUFFINS

On my travels I have found that Americans and New Zealanders have all been mad about muffins. They feature on breakfast menus, for brunch buffets, for afternoon teas and often for supper! They can actually be very versatile, good with soups, or with vegetables.

This basic recipe makes four but you have to use the special muffin tins which measure about 3 in (7.5 cm) across and 1¾ in (4 cm) high. They need to be lined with similarly sized paper cake cases.

4 oz (100 g) self-raising flour

1 level teaspoon baking powder

a pinch of salt

2 oz (50 g) granulated sugar

5 fl oz (150 ml) milk

2 tablespoons light-flavoured oil of choice (I normally use sunflower)

1 medium egg

FLAVOURINGS (SWEET)

2 oz (50 g) fresh berries (e.g. blueberries, raspberries) or chocolate chips

FLAVOURINGS (SAVOURY)

2 oz (50 g) sweetcorn kernels and a pinch of curry powder

or

2 oz (50 g) honey-coated salted peanuts, roughly chopped

or

1 oz (25 g) each of finely chopped red pepper and fennel

or

2 oz (50 g) finely diced onion cooked in a non-stick pan until quite dark, nigh burnt

Pre-heat the oven to 200°C/400°F/Gas 6.

Combine the dry ingredients in a bowl, and in a separate bowl lightly beat together the milk, oil and egg. Fold your chosen flavouring agent, sweet or savoury, into the dry mix, then combine the milk mix with the flour mix. It will be very runny.

Divide the mix between your four cake cases and bake in the pre-heated oven for 30 minutes. The muffins are best served warm.

Muffins
(page 71)

My
Salade
Niçoise
(page 70)

Yorkshire
Pudding
with
Onion
Gravy
(page 70)

FILLED PANCAKES

Pancakes make for perfect party pieces as they are so very versatile, and can be used as starter, main course or pud. Two per person would make a wonderful starter; three would be a main course, served with a salad.

The pancakes can be prepared a few days in advance, and the following mixture will make twelve to fourteen pancakes using a non-stick, 6 in (15 cm) frying pan. The fillings listed are sufficient to cover a half side of *four* pancakes. By folding rather then rolling them up, they appear to be larger, and they also take more filling.

4 oz (100 g) plain flour, sieved

a pinch of salt

2 medium eggs, lightly beaten

5 fl oz (150 ml) cold water

5 fl oz (150 ml) cold milk

2 tablespoons olive oil

a little butter for cooking

filling of choice (following)

Sieve the flour into a bowl with the salt and make a well in the middle. Into this pour the lightly beaten egg, and the water, milk and oil. Using a beater, beat away until you get a smooth, thin batter. Cover with cling film and chill for at least an hour.

When you wish to cook, liberally paint the base and sides of your frying pan with a little butter (I use about ½ teaspoon melted butter per 6 in/15 cm pancake),

and pour in sufficient batter to very lightly coat the whole base of the pan. Initially you might put in too much but this does not matter as it is a relatively simple task to pour the surplus back into your bowl of batter. Practice will make perfect. It is important that the pan is really hot each time you start to make a pancake. A minute is all that is required (at the most) for cooking, and by sliding a palette knife under one corner you will see how the batter has formed a smooth, silk-like texture, and has turned golden. If the mix was thin enough, you won't need to cook the other side. Turn out on to a square of greaseproof paper and continue with the next pancake, piling them all up, interleaved with greaseproof paper. If you are not going to use them immediately, wrap them (with the paper) in a lightly dampened tea towel.

Pre-heat oven to 180°C/350°F/Gas 4.

When you wish to serve, fill each pancake with some of the chosen filling, and fold over as described above to a half-moon shape. Place on a lightly buttered baking tray and put into the pre-heated oven. They will take 12 minutes to heat through. Serve immediately.

LAMB BOLOGNESE AND BOURSIN FILLING

4 tablespoons My Bolognese (see page 119)

1 x 3¼ oz (80 g) packet Boursin cream cheese

Make this pancake filling when you have some leftover Bolognese. Simply bring the meat and cheese together lightly.

TOMATO AND AVOCADO FILLING

1 x 14 oz (397 g) tin chopped tomatoes with basil

1 ripe avocado, peeled, stoned and diced

½ teaspoon curry powder (optional)

Reduce the tomatoes gently by half to form a thick paste, then combine with the diced avocado and curry powder if using (this latter enhances the flavours).

SPINACH, WATERCRESS, HAZELNUT AND MASCARPONE FILLING

4 oz (100 g) young spinach, very finely chopped

4 oz (100 g) watercress, very finely chopped

4 oz (100 g) ground hazelnuts

1 teaspoon oil of choice (hazelnut would be interesting)

8 teaspoons Mascarpone cheese

Put all the ingredients into a pan over a high heat and stir together with a wooden spoon: a ball of filling will be made in just over a minute. When cold, divide it between the pancakes.

AIR-DRIED HAM, ASPARAGUS AND MUSTARD FILLING

20 very small asparagus tips

4 tablespoons oil of choice

2 tablespoons balsamic vinegar

4 teaspoons coarse-grain mustard

4 x ½ oz (15 g) slices air-dried ham

Fry the asparagus tips in the oil for 3–5 minutes (they will still be pretty firm), then add the vinegar. Immediately remove from the heat and stir in the mustard. When the asparagus is cold, wrap each slice of ham round five pieces of asparagus and put in the pancake.

SAUSAGEMEAT WITH APRICOT FILLING

8 oz (225 g) sausagemeat, broken into small pieces

2 tablespoons oil of choice

8 dried apricots, very finely diced

2 teaspoons brandy

salt and freshly ground black pepper

Cook the sausagemeat in the oil until broken up and cooked through, about 3–4 minutes. Add the apricots, brandy and seasoning and cook for a further minute to soften the apricots. When cool, divide between the pancakes.

BANANA AND MANGO FILLING

4 oz (100 g) banana, peeled and finely cubed

4 oz (100 g) mango, peeled, stoned and finely diced

Simply mix together. You can add a dessertspoon of dark rum if you like.

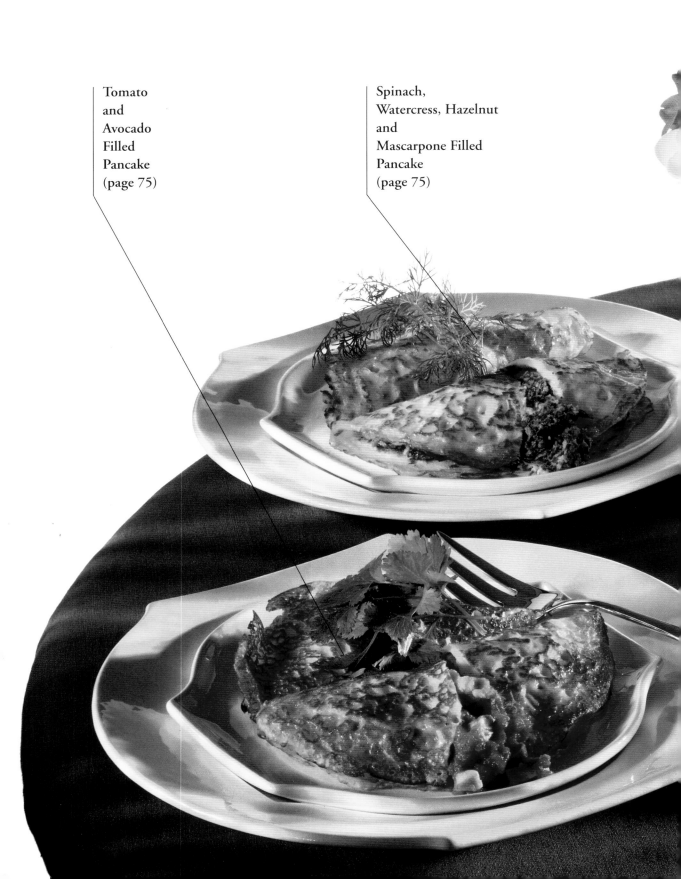

Tomato
and
Avocado
Filled
Pancake
(page 75)

Spinach,
Watercress, Hazelnut
and
Mascarpone Filled
Pancake
(page 75)

Banana
and
Mango
Filled
Pancake
(page 75)

SIMPLY
Splendid
MAIN COURSES

BAKED HERBED TROUT

An unusual flavour with trout – that of honey – but try it!

4 trout, gutted but still with heads and tails on

2 large sprigs fresh rosemary

8 sage leaves

4 oz (100 g) butter, melted

4 tablespoons honey

Pre-heat the oven to 180°C/350°F/Gas 4.

Wash the fish well and pat dry on kitchen paper. Open out the bellies of the fish and insert the herbs, dividing them evenly. Lay the trout on a flat baking tray and paint with about 40 g (1½ oz) of the butter. Bake in the pre-heated oven for 12 minutes only.

Whilst the fish are cooking, bring together the remaining melted butter and the honey. Pour over the trout just prior to serving.

BAKED TROUT WITH ALMONDS

A more conventional combination, but the *two* types of almond used add textural and visual interest.

4 fillets of fresh trout, taken from 2 fresh fish, skinned

2 oz (50 g) butter, melted

2 oz (50 g) ground almonds

2 oz (50 g) flaked almonds

1 large lemon, cut into 4 wedges

4 sprigs fresh parsley

Pre-heat the oven to 180°C/350°F/Gas 4.

Wash the prepared fillets and pat dry on kitchen paper. Use a little of the butter to coat the base of an appropriately sized baking tray then brush each side of the prepared fillets with the balance. Dunk one side of each fillet in the ground almonds and then arrange, almond side down, on the baking tray. Scatter the flaked almonds over the top of the fillets.

Bake in the oven for 12 minutes only, then serve garnished with the lemon wedges and parsley.

Baked
Herbed
Trout
(page 79)

Baked
Trout
with
Almonds
(page 79)

Marinated Cubed
Salmon
(page 82)
on
Purée of Celeriac
(page 146)

MARINATED CUBED SALMON ON PUREE OF CELERIAC

You could offer a purée of potatoes instead of the celeriac (see page 139), but I like the combination of flavours of the marinated salmon and celeriac.

2 x 5 oz (150 g) fillets of salmon, skinned and cubed

a little butter for greasing the tray

MARINADE

rind and juice of 2 oranges

1 tablespoon light soy sauce

2 garlic cloves, peeled and crushed

2 nuggets ginger preserved in syrup, finely grated

TO SERVE

Purée of Celeriac (see page 146)

Combine all the marinade ingredients in a suitable dish and marinate the salmon cubes, covered and chilled, for two days.

When you wish to cook, pre-heat the oven to 240°C/475°F/Gas 9. Spread the salmon cubes over a lightly buttered baking tray in four circles, and cook for 12 minutes only.

Meanwhile make (or reheat) the Purée of Celeriac. Arrange this on four plates and serve the salmon cubes on top.

COD WITH HOT VINAIGRETTE

Cod is a much maligned fish. On more than one occasion at Miller Howe I have heard diners remark, 'Oh God, cod at *these* prices!' But then, when the chef goes around the tables, they exclaim, 'I didn't know cod could be so delicious!'

Start the preparation for this dish at least 8 hours beforehand, and virtually all you have to do thereafter in the evening is pre-heat the oven.

4 x 6 oz (175 g) fillets of cod, skinned

10 fl oz (300 ml) dry white wine

a little butter for greasing the tray

VINAIGRETTE

4 tablespoons oil of choice

1 tablespoon white wine vinegar

a pinch each of dry English mustard powder, salt, white pepper and sugar

1 teaspoon lemon juice

freshly ground coriander seeds

Marinate your skinned fillets for at least 8 hours in the white wine.

Make the vinaigrette by mixing everything together well, adding freshly ground coriander seeds (grind them in a pepper grinder) to taste. (If you double or treble the quantity, but always keeping the proportions of four parts oil to one of vinegar, it will keep well, and it's handy to have around.)

When ready to cook, pre-heat the oven to 180°C/350°F/Gas 4.

Pat the fillets dry and place on a lightly buttered baking tray. They will take 5 minutes only to cook in the pre-heated oven. Meanwhile warm through the vinaigrette very gently. Serve the fish with a little of the hot vinaigrette. Some Garlic Puréed Potatoes (see page 139) would be nice as well.

Cod with
Hot Vinaigrette
(page 82)
with
Garlic Puréed Potatoes
(page 139)

Baked Pesto Cod
(page 86)
with
Baked Potato
Circles
(page 134)

BAKED PESTO COD

Fish is becoming more popular these days, but you have to seek out a supplier who does, in fact, sell *fresh* fish, and not items that have been deep-frozen and then slowly thawed out.

4 x 6 oz (175 g) fillets of cod, skinned

8 teaspoons Pesto Sauce (see page 55)

a little butter for greasing the tray

1 lemon, cut into 4 wedges

4 sprigs fresh parsley

Place the fillets on your work surface, and cover the top side with the pesto. Place on a buttered tray and chill until you wish to cook.

Pre-heat the oven to 200°C/400°F/ Gas 6.

Bake the fish in the pre-heated oven for 6 minutes only. Serve on warm plates garnished with the lemon wedges and parsley. A good accompaniment is the Baked Potato Circles on page 134.

SALMON FISHCAKES

These fishcakes can be prepared – even cooked – the day before, and chilled until ready to heat through.

8 oz (225 g) potatoes, peeled, cooked and plainly mashed (see page 139)

12 oz (350 g) raw salmon fillet, minced

1 medium egg yolk

1 heaped tablespoon bought or home-made mayonnaise (see page 21)

1 teaspoon tomato paste

1 teaspoon snipped chives

1½ tablespoons chopped parsley

4 heaped tablespoons fine fresh breadcrumbs

salt and freshly ground black pepper

1 tablespoon olive oil

1 oz (25 g) soft butter

Combine the mashed potatoes with the salmon, egg yolk, mayonnaise, tomato paste and herbs in a large bowl, and then divide into four portions. Shape as for rissoles and lightly coat with the well seasoned breadcrumbs. Put on a baking tray, cover with cling film and leave to chill. Do this the day before the meal. You can even *fry* them the day before.

Fry two at a time in a small frying-pan in the oil and butter; replenish this if necessary as you fry the next two cakes. Cook until quite brown on each side. Transfer back to the baking tray and when cold cover again and leave somewhere cool.

When you want to serve the fishcakes, pre-heat the oven to 180°C/350°F/Gas 4. Re-heat the fishcakes for 12–15 minutes. Serve with Tomato Sauce (see page 39), if liked.

Tuna
Pasta
(page 90)

Salmon
Fishcake
(page 87)

TUNA PASTA

This has to be my very favourite meal when I am feeling fed up to the back teeth about working on and with food!

2 tablespoons oil of choice

2 oz (50 g) soft butter

12 oz (350 g) onions, peeled and finely sliced

1 x 8 oz (225 g) tin baked beans of choice

1 x 8 oz (225 g) tin tuna of choice, drained well

12 oz (350 g) dried macaroni or tagliatelli

salt and freshly ground black pepper

TO SERVE

2 hard-boiled eggs

4 generous tablespoons finely chopped parsley

4 dessertspoons crème fraîche

Heat the oil and butter in a frying pan and cook the onion until well browned, about 10 minutes. Add the beans and drained tuna, and gently heat through.

Meanwhile cook the pasta in boiling salted water according to the packet instructions. Drain well, and divide between your four warmed plates. Do the same with the fish and bean mix. Push the eggs quickly through a sieve and scatter over the top of each portion, along with the parsley. Top off with the *crème fraîche* and freshly ground black pepper.

SAVOURY SOLE WITH AVOCADO AND AIR-DRIED HAM

These rolled fillets of sole can be served warm or cold. They can be presented whole, or sliced and fanned out on the plate so that the various colours can be seen. You could accompany them with a Cream Sauce made with cider (see page 47), a delicious addition.

4 x 6 oz (175 g) fillets of lemon sole, skinned

4 thin slices air-dried ham

1 ripe avocado, peeled, quartered and stoned

4 teaspoons olive oil

Lie the slices of air-dried ham flat on your work surface and place your sole fillets, skinned side up, on top of these. Put a quarter of avocado in the middle and then wrap the fish and ham round it. Cut four large squares of cooking cling-film and in the middle of each put a teaspoon of olive oil. Transfer your rolled-up fish to this and then bring the top of the cling film down over the prepared fish, and the bottom up and over. Holding the two other ends, by twirling you will form something resembling a Christmas cracker. Chill until needed.

When you wish to cook, pre-heat the oven to 180°C/350°F/Gas 4. Put the fish parcels on a cooling rack in a small roasting tray full of boiling water, and bake in the oven for 12 minutes only. They are easy to slide out of the cling film, and they will have kept their smooth shape.

Stuffed
Sole
Baked
in
Cider
(page 94)

Battered Monkfish
(page 95) with deep-fried
leeks on a bed of
Buttered Caraway
Cabbage
(page 143)

Savoury Sole
with
Avocado
and
Air-dried Ham
(page 91)

STUFFED SOLE
BAKED IN CIDER

A rolled sole recipe, using mushrooms in the stuffing, and the wonderful flavour of cider. A dry one is best.

4 x 6 oz (175 g) fillets of fresh sole, skinned

2 oz (50 g) butter

2 oz (50 g) onions, peeled and finely chopped

4 oz (100 g) fresh mushrooms, finely sliced

salt and freshly ground black pepper

5 fl oz (150 ml) cider of choice

2 level tablespoons chopped parsley

Melt the butter in a frying pan and cook the onions until golden, about 8 minutes. Add the mushrooms and cook for 5 more minutes. Using a slotted spoon, transfer the vegetables to kitchen paper to drain.

Lay the sole fillets skinned side up on your work surface and season them well. Divide the fried mixture between the fillets, placing it at one end, then roll each fillet up into a sausage shape around the filling. (Use a wooden cocktail stick to hold them if necessary.)

Put the juices from the frying pan into a small casserole, lay the prepared fish rolls in this, and cover with the cider. At this stage the dish can be rested in the fridge, for at least 4 hours.

When ready to cook, pre-heat the oven to 180°C/350°F/Gas 4. Bake the sole rolls for 15 minutes only. Transfer to hot plates, pour the juices over, and sprinkle each portion with the freshly chopped parsley.

BATTERED MONKFISH

You will have quite a lot of the batter left over, but as it is virtually impossible to use half a fresh egg, this is the only way I can produce this method. But the batter is ideal for most deep-frying, in particular for sprays of fresh sage or basil, to be used as an edible garnish.

4 x 6 oz (175 g) fillets of monkfish, skinned and boned

oil of choice for deep-frying

salt and freshly ground black pepper

BATTER

8 oz (225 g) plain white flour

1 medium egg, lightly beaten

15 fl oz (450 ml) cold water plus 1 tablespoon

For the batter, simply mix all together, using a hand beater to make a smooth paste. No lumps please. (I know the tablespoon of water sounds very finicky, but it does make all the difference.)

Simply dunk each monkfish fillet into the batter and then drop at once into the pre-heated deep-fryer at 180°C/350°F. Cook for 6 minutes only.

Take out and transfer to a double thickness of kitchen paper to drain well. Sprinkle with salt and freshly ground black pepper and serve at once. It's ideal with the Tomato Sauce on page 39, or the Mustard Dressing on page 21; it's also delicious accompanied by the Buttered Caraway Cabbage on page 143.

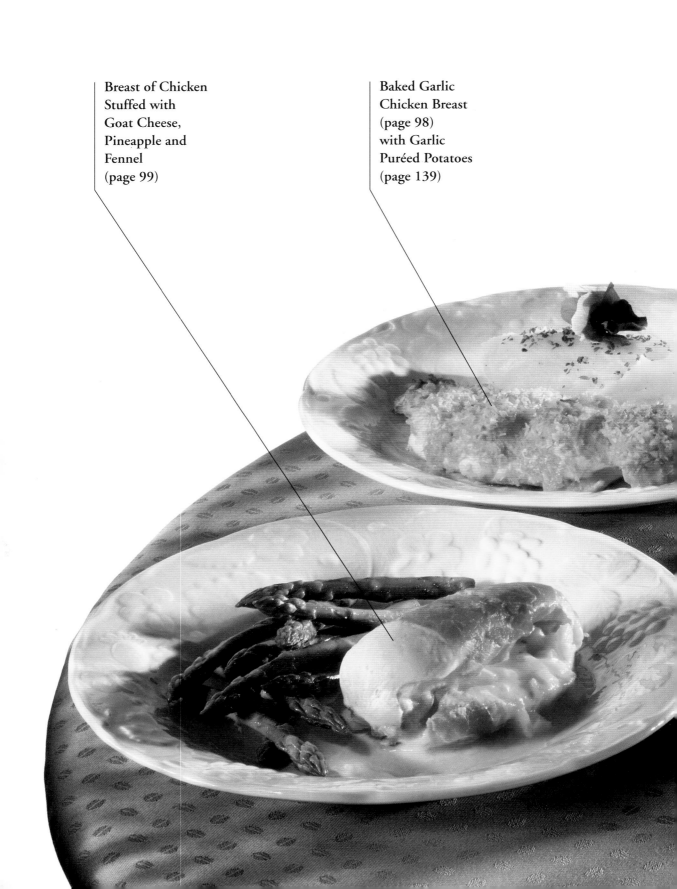

Breast of Chicken
Stuffed with
Goat Cheese,
Pineapple and
Fennel
(page 99)

Baked Garlic
Chicken Breast
(page 98)
with Garlic
Puréed Potatoes
(page 139)

Tropical
Chicken
Stir-fry
(page 98)
on pasta

TROPICAL CHICKEN STIR-FRY

This is a quick dish I frequently do when on holiday out in the sunny Cape. It is slightly sweet but goes well with a few bottles of well chilled light white or rosé wine.

1 lb (450 g) skinned and boned chicken breasts, cubed

10 fl oz (300 ml) coconut milk

2 bananas

1 mango

4 tablespoons garlic oil

2 tablespoons chopped parsley

Marinate the chicken cubes in the coconut milk for at least 4 hours.

Peel the bananas and mango, and remove the large flat stone from the latter. Cut both into similar small pieces. Do this just before cooking.

Using a large frying pan heat the oil until smoking, and then throw in the strained chicken cubes. Stir-fry for 5 minutes, then fold in the banana and mango cubes, and cook for a further 4–5 minutes.

Scatter on a generous sprinkling of chopped parsley and serve with either pasta, rice or the Garlic Puréed Potatoes on page 139.

BAKED GARLIC CHICKEN BREAST

This recipe really is appealing in its simplicity. In fact it's *so* easy, it could even be aspired to by a four-year-old in the kitchen.

4 chicken breasts, skinned and boned

a little butter for greasing the tray

4 tablespoons Garlic Tomato Dressing (see page 21)

4 dessertspoons fine breadcrumbs, crumbed cornflakes or desiccated coconut

Pre-heat the oven to 180°C/350°F/Gas 4.

Lay the four skinned chicken breasts on a lightly buttered tray. Coat each with a generous tablespoon of the dressing, and then on top of this spread a dessertspoon of breadcrumbs, cornflakes or coconut.

Bake in the oven for 20 minutes, then finish off for less than a minute under a hot grill. The chicken is both moist and flavoursome, and slightly crisp on top.

BREAST OF CHICKEN STUFFED WITH GOAT CHEESE, PINEAPPLE AND FENNEL

An easy and tasty chicken dish. Start preparation at least 12 hours in advance – the marination in the cider makes all the difference.

4 chicken breasts, skinned and boned

300 ml (10 fl oz) dry cider

4 oz (100 g) good goat cheese, coarsely grated

4 oz (100 g) pineapple flesh, finely diced

4 oz (100 g) fennel, finely diced

4 slices air-dried ham

olive oil

TO SERVE

Cream Sauce (see page 47), made with the retained cider

2 tablespoons chopped chives

Marinate the chicken breasts in the cider for at least 12 hours. Cover with cling film and leave in the fridge or a cool place. Remove from the cider – which you keep for the sauce – and pat dry on kitchen paper.

For the filling, mix the cheese, pineapple and fennel together. Divide into four equal piles.

Make an incision in the underside of each chicken breast sufficient in size to take the cheese mixture, fill with the mixture, and then wrap each breast in a slice of ham. Lightly paint four squares of cooking cling film with olive oil and put the chicken breasts on these, easing the cling film up and over. Pour 1 dessertspoon of cider on top of each breast, and then tie up like a boiled sweet. Chill until ready to cook.

When you wish to cook, pre-heat the oven to 180°C/350°F/Gas 4. Get a small roasting tray, and put a cooling rack on top. Half fill the roasting tray with boiling water. Place the four 'parcels' on the rack and bake in the pre-heated oven for 25 minutes.

Meanwhile make the sauce, using the remaining cider, reduced to 2 tablespoons. When ready to serve, remove the parcels from the oven, and the breasts from the cling film. Place on warm plates and serve with the sauce into which you have stirred the chives at the last moment.

Roast Chicken
with Mascarpone,
Garlic,
Sage and
Orange
(page 102)

Apricot
Stuffing
(page 102)

Peppered
Orange
Duck
Breasts
(page 103)

ROAST CHICKEN WITH MASCARPONE, GARLIC, SAGE AND ORANGE

Initially this might sound a mouthful but, believe you me, it is a delicious mouthful, and so easy to do.

1 x 3 lb (1.4 kg) fresh free-range chicken

8 oz (225 g) Mascarpone cheese

2 teaspoons garlic paste

16 fresh sage leaves, chopped

finely grated rind and juice of 2 oranges

4 slices smoked bacon

Ease the skin away from the flesh of both chicken breasts and drumsticks. Mix the Mascarpone with the garlic paste, sage and orange rind, and put into a piping bag. Pipe half over each side of the chicken, including the legs, *between* flesh and skin. Put into your roasting tin and cover with cling film if not being cooked at once.

Pre-heat the oven to 190°C/375°F/Gas 5.

Pour the orange juice over the bird, and then put the bacon slices on the breasts. Cook for 1 hour. Take the crisp bacon off the top, and lower the temperature of the oven to 160°C/325°F/Gas 3, and cook for a further 30 minutes.

The bird needs no gravy or sauce as it is extremely moist. Portion the two breasts and drumsticks on to the crisp bacon, and serve with Garlic Puréed Potatoes (see page 139) if you like.

You can, if you wish, when the chicken has cooked for 1½ hours, take it out of the roasting tray and wrap it in foil. Transfer the tin with its juices to your warm hob and stir in dry English mustard powder, horseradish cream, lemon juice or vinegar according to taste, and serve this as a light sauce. (I have also used redcurrant jelly, a little balsamic vinegar or, on one occasion, some soft peanut butter!)

APRICOT STUFFING

I had to include this new stuffing, as it is so delicious. Cook alongside your roast chicken or turkey, in a separate dish. It would also go well with pork.

4 oz (100 g) dried apricots

2 tablespoons brandy

8 oz (225 g) onions, peeled and finely chopped

4 oz (100 g) smoked bacon, rinded and finely chopped

4 oz (100 g) butter

12 oz (350 g) pork sausagemeat

2 oz (50 g) fresh breadcrumbs

Soak the apricots overnight in the brandy to plump them up. Chop the apricots coarsely, and retain any brandy.

Fry the onion and bacon in the butter until soft, then stir in the apricots, brandy (if any) and sausagemeat. Simmer for 15 minutes, stirring to brown the sausagemeat. Fold in the breadcrumbs and transfer to a suitable dish. Cool, then chill until ready to cook.

When you wish to eat, pre-heat the oven to 180°C/350°F/Gas 4 and bake for 30 minutes. Or simply add to the oven in which the meat or bird which it will accompany is cooking, and cook for 30 minutes.

PEPPERED ORANGE DUCK BREASTS

If you like peppered steaks (see page 111), I hope you will like this variation, as it is a new favourite of mine. Duck breasts are now available in many outlets, presented off the bone in individual vacuum packs with the very minimum of fat.

4 individual duck breasts

juice and rind of 2 oranges

oil of choice

2 tablespoons pink peppercorns

2 tablespoons black peppercorns

4 oz (100 g) soft butter

4 tablespoons Apple Purée (see page 122)

Remove the skin and any fat from each duck breast and cut the skin into very thin strips. Leave to one side. Marinate the skinned breasts in the orange juice and rind in a covered dish for at least 24 hours.

Remove the breasts from the dish, dry on kitchen paper, then paint with a little oil of choice. Mix the two types of peppercorns together and crush coarsely. Sieve to get rid of the hot 'dust', then coat each breast in some of the mixed crushed peppercorns left in the sieve.

In a dry frying pan cook off the skin strips until quite crisp, then put to one side. Heat through 4 tablespoons of the oil and then add the soft butter. When nice and hot put in the prepared duck breasts and cook for 5 minutes on each side, which will give you portions that are not bloody!

Add the remaining orange juice to the Apple Purée, heat through gently, then put on a warm plate with the breast on top. Sprinkle with the rich, crisp bits of duck skin.

Apple
Chutney
(page 42)

Casseroled
Belly Pork
with
Pumpkin
(page 108)
 and carrots

Raised
Pork
Pie
(page 107)

Braised
Pork
Chops
(page 106)

BRAISED PORK CHOPS

A simple and delicious dish, but it must be started at least 24 hours in advance so that the pork chops can be flavoured and tenderised by the wine.

4 x 8 oz (225 g) pork chops on the bone

10 fl oz (300 ml) dry white wine

2 tablespoons oil of choice

8 teaspoons coarse-grain mustard

4 teaspoons runny honey

16 fresh sage leaves

Marinate the chops for 24 hours in the dry white wine in a suitable container, covered with cling film.

Pre-heat the oven to 150°C/300°F/ Gas 2.

Remove the chops from the wine, retaining the wine, and pat dry on kitchen paper. Heat the oil in a very hot, small frying pan, and seal the chops one by one on both sides. Each time you put a chop in or turn it over you should get a loud hissing noise from the oil. If this doesn't happen, your oil was not hot enough and you will not seal the juices in properly.

Remove the chops from the frying pan and spread 2 teaspoons mustard and 1 teaspoon honey over both sides of each chop. Place in a casserole which can hold the four chops side by side. Pour over the wine in which they marinated, and put 4 sage leaves on top of every chop.

Bake in the pre-heated oven for 2 hours. You can then, if you like, take the chops out of their juices and wine, and put aside on a tray covered with foil. It will take about 4 minutes to reduce the juices which could be served as a sauce, but the chops are lovely, moist and tender as they are.

RAISED PORK PIE

I was one of the first of many (so I am now told) to bombard British Rail with complaining letters as soon as they decided to withdraw pork pies from sale. It was done, according to my first reply, for health reasons and because of a fall in sales. What rubbish! They are now back on the trolleys, and the assistants tell me they are once again one of their bestsellers.

The pies can be made the night before, as they are served cold.

8 oz (225 g) plain flour

1 teaspoon salt

½ nutmeg, finely grated

1 level teaspoon dry English mustard powder

3 tablespoons cold water

2 tablespoons milk

3 oz (75 g) lard

FILLING

6 oz (175 g) pork sausagemeat

1 tablespoon pine kernels, toasted (see page 55)

1 medium egg, lightly beaten

1 level dessertspoon pink peppercorns (optional), finely crushed

salt and freshly ground black pepper

1 tablespoon chopped parsley

Pre-heat the oven to 200°C/400°F/Gas 6, and have ready four muffin tins, 3 in (7.5 cm) across, and 1¾ in (4 cm) high.

Make the filling first. Simply mix all the ingredients together.

To make the pastry, sieve the flour, salt, nutmeg and mustard into your mixing bowl. Bring the water and milk to the boil along with the lard, and when melted pour immediately on to the flour. Using the bread dough hook, knead to a smooth ball. (You can do it by hand, it's just hard work. You've also got to work extremely quickly.)

Divide the dough into five pieces. Put one ball of dough on the base of each muffin tin. With your thumb and first finger, ease the dough up round the sides. Divide the filling between the pastry cups. Roll out the fifth piece of dough and cut into lids. Fit these on top of the filling and, using the back of a fork, secure the lids to the bases. Paint with a little extra oil, then rest in the fridge for 2 hours.

Bake in the oven for 20 minutes, lower the oven temperature to 180°C/350°F/ Gas 4 and cook for a further 20 minutes. Remove from the oven and cool.

Serve cold with the Apple Chutney on page 42.

CASSEROLED BELLY
PORK WITH PUMPKIN

Folk frequently turn up their noses when they see this cut of meat in the market. I can remember when, desperately poor but happy, slaving away in Her Majesty's weekly repertory theatre in Barrow, I had to do the thrice-weekly shopping. As the market was about to close, I would realise with sheer delight that I could get this particular joint at an even lower price than normal. The joys of smelling it cooking, seeing it on the plate and anticipating the devouring were enough to get my salivary glands going.

If you like, serve the following casserole with simple baked potatoes, a dish that is ideal for Hallowe'en, Guy Fawkes Night or any winter evening.

1½ lb (675 g) skinned belly pork,
off the bone

salt and freshly ground black pepper

1 oz (25 g) soft butter

4 oz (100 g) onions, peeled and finely diced

2 juicy garlic cloves, peeled and crushed to a
fine paste with a little salt

1 lb (450 g) pumpkin, peeled and
finely diced

5 fl oz (150 ml) apple juice

16 fresh sage leaves, roughly chopped

Get your butcher to slice the belly pork into ½ in (1 cm) rashers.

Pre-heat the oven to 200°C/400°F/ Gas 6.

Lightly season the prepared pork slices and seal each slice on both sides in a hot non-stick frying pan without using any oil or butter. Put to one side.

Melt the butter in a large pan and brown the onion along with the garlic paste, about 6 minutes. Add the pumpkin and apple juice and season generously with freshly ground black pepper. Stir well.

Spread the pumpkin mixture into a suitable casserole and sprinkle with the chopped sage. Lay the sealed pork strips on top. Cover with foil and cook in the pre-heated oven for 30 minutes. Remove the foil and cook for a further 10 minutes. Serve hot.

SAVOURY BEEF OLIVES

These beef olives, with two varying stuffings, make quite a substantial main course if served on a large baked croûton (see page 64).

8 x 2½ oz (65 g) very thin slices of best fillet of beef

10 fl oz (300 ml) dry white wine

4 tablespoons oil of choice

BLACK PUDDING STUFFING

4 oz (100 g) black pudding

2 oz (50 g) onions, peeled and chopped

1 teaspoon garlic paste

15 fresh sage leaves

freshly ground black pepper

1 teaspoon walnut oil

CHICKEN STUFFING

4 oz (100 g) chicken breast, skinned and diced

2 oz (50 g) onions, peeled and chopped

2 small mushrooms

2 teaspoons finely chopped fresh thyme

½ teaspoon garlic paste

4 sun-dried tomatoes, chopped

Place the beef fillet slices between two pieces of lightly oiled cling film and beat even thinner. Place in a dish (cling film removed) and cover with the wine. Leave to marinate for at least 24 hours.

To make the beef olive stuffings, put all the ingredients of both – separately, of course – in the food processor and process to a fine mince texture.

Lay four of the marinated fillet slices on your work surfaces and divide the black pudding mix between them. Fold over the long sides and roll up into a firm sausage. Repeat with the four remaining fillet slices and the chicken stuffing.

Pre-heat the oven to 200°C/400°F/ Gas 6.

In a small 7 in (18 cm) frying pan, heat a tablespoon of oil until hot. Seal two olives at a time in the oil, then place on a lightly greased baking tray. This only takes a couple of minutes. Do all eight, using more oil, and remembering to make sure you know which are which! Bake all together for 8 minutes only in the pre-heated oven. Serve immediately.

You can stop at the frying stage and leave the olives to go cold. In the oven pre-heated to the same temperature as above, from cold they will take 12 minutes to cook.

ROAST BEEF

People catering for four or fewer diners are always deprived of roast beef, for in no way do I think you can properly roast a joint weighing less than 4 lb (1.8 kg). Roast beef may seem out of place in this book of simple and fairly fast suppers, but I often cook this for my *own* supper and find it no hardship to finish off the cold slices either with a salad or simply in sandwiches.

This is a perfectly foolproof way of cooking rolled beef, and it goes well with the Yorkshire Pudding and Onion Gravy on page 70. Needless to say, the butcher should have hung the meat for at least three weeks, and in no way should the initial joint look pink and fresh.

1 x 4 lb (1.8 kg) piece of beef, weighed after boning

oil of choice

freshly ground black pepper

Pre-heat the oven to 240°C/475°F/Gas 9.

Your friendly butcher should have boned, trimmed and rolled the beef, and tied it at about 1½ in (4 cm) intervals with string. Rub a good oil gently all over the joint, sprinkle with pepper, then put in your roasting tray, fat side up.

Cook the beef in the pre-heated oven for 20 minutes, then reduce the oven temperature to 190°C/375°F/Gas 5, and roast for a further 45 minutes if you like rare beef. I personally don't, so I cook mine for 1–1¼ hours instead of 45 minutes.

At the end of this time, remove the joint from the oven and wrap in a double thickness of foil. Leave to rest in a warm part of the kitchen for 10–15 minutes, then carve.

GRILLED PEPPERED STEAKS

There are cars and cars – Rolls Royces and Reliant Robins. Likewise with steaks. It is so important to root out a good butcher who himself knows what to look for when he is buying the carcasses and who will take the time and trouble to hang them for at least three weeks. Here in the little village of Crawshawbooth we are well served by the Riley family who still raise their own animals on their hilltop farm, slaughter weekly and hang sensibly but, more important still, *care* for their produce all along the line. They have never, ever, let me down, but then I always let them know my requirements well in advance.

However, the success of this dish ultimately depends on the heat your grill produces. Many electric so-called grills on modern electric stoves never get up to a really hot, hot heat, but you do have a better chance with gas. However, having only electricity here at the farm I find that I have to switch mine on to full power for at least 30–40 minutes beforehand. This might sound both daft and uneconomical, but immediately you put the steaks under the grill you want them to be sealed pronto to keep in the luscious natural juices, and the oil that has started to soak through, thus producing juicy and tender lumps of meat. Another mistake many people have made when grilling is putting salt on the meat prior to cooking: this draws the juices *out*, quite the reverse of what you want.

4 well-hung sirloin steaks, between 8 and 10 oz (225–300 g) each

olive oil

4 level tablespoons pink or black peppercorns, coarsely crushed with a pestle and mortar, then sieved (see page 103)

2 level teaspoons garlic paste

salt

TO SERVE

Balsamic Onions (see page 130)

Paint each side of the prepared steaks thoroughly with the olive oil and put on to a cooling rack with a baking tray underneath. Cover with foil and leave to marinate for at least 4 hours. This can be done in the morning, or even the night before, leaving the steaks in the fridge.

A good half hour before you wish to cook, pre-heat the grill to its hottest temperature.

Meanwhile on one side of each steak press some of the crushed peppercorns left in the sieve. Place peppercorns down on a baking tray, painting the other side with the garlic paste. For medium done steaks, grill each side for 4 minutes about 1 in (2.5 cm) away from the grill itself. Turn with tongs, never a fork.

Sprinkle on a little salt before serving, on top of the warmed through Balsamic Onions. Another lovely accompaniment is a scaled-down version of the Cabbage Pizza on page 126.

Savoury
Beef Olives
(page 109)
with
Purée of Celeriac
(page 146)

Grilled
Peppered Steaks
(page 111)
with
Asparagus Parcels
(page 143)

Roast Beef
(page 110)
and Yorkshire Pudding
with
Onion Gravy
(page 70)

MUTTON PIE WITH CHESTNUT, WATERCRESS, APRICOT AND GINGER

A delicious pie with a multitude of less usual flavours. Both the pastry and the chestnuts can be prepared the day before, but try to make the pie at the last minute to serve fresh and hot.

PIE PASTRY

12 oz (350 g) plain flour

9 oz (250 g) very soft butter

1 medium egg

1 tablespoon fresh lemon juice

FILLING

8 oz (225 g) fresh chestnuts (not dried)

1½ lb (675 g) lean shoulder of lamb, cubed

1 pint (600 ml) lamb stock (bought or home-made)

4 oz (100 g) dried apricots, cut into small pieces

2 nuggets ginger preserved in syrup, roughly chopped

1 bunch watercress, roughly chopped

freshly ground black pepper

1 large egg, beaten

Have ready a loose-bottomed flan tin, 8 in (20 cm) in diameter and about 1½ in (4 cm) deep.

For the pie pastry, sieve the flour on to your work surface. Make a well in the centre and into this put your very soft butter. On to this break the egg and add the fresh lemon juice. Using your finger ends, tap the egg and lemon carefully into the butter and then, using a palette knife, bring the flour over and on to the butter mix. By cutting through sharply and continuously, you make the pastry. Divide the dough into two balls, wrap each loosely in cling film, and leave to chill.

When you wish to bake the pie base, take out one ball of pastry and allow it to come round to the same texture as when it was first made. Roll out and use to cover the base and sides of the loose-bottomed flan tin. Line with foil and baking beans, and chill.

Pre-heat the oven to 160°C/325°F/Gas 3. Bake the pie base blind for 30–40 minutes. When the foil and beans are removed, the pastry case should be as crisp as a cream cracker.

Try to prepare and cook the chestnuts in advance as well. Nick each one with the tip of a sharp knife, and place on a baking tray. Bake in the oven pre-heated to 200°C/400°F/Gas 6 for 1 hour. Remove, cool a little, then take off the shells and inner flaky skin. Quarter the nuts.

When you want to cook the pie, pre-heat the oven to 190°C/375°F/Gas 5.

To cook the pie filling, simmer the cubed lamb in the lamb stock, making sure that you *do* simmer on your hob (it must never boil or bubble), about 1 hour.

Strain the lamb, return the stock to the heat, and reduce this to 5 fl oz (150 ml). Put the cooked lamb in a mixing bowl and mix with the chestnut quarters, the apricots, ginger, watercress and lots of pepper. Bind with most of the egg, and turn into the cold cooked flan case. Pour on the reduced stock.

Using the balance of the pastry – remember, it must be soft when you come to roll it – roll out a lid, and attach firmly to the base of the pie. Decorate as you will. Paint the top with the remaining beaten egg, and bake in the pre-heated oven for 35 minutes. Serve hot.

ROAST SHOULDER OF LAMB WITH GARLIC AND ANCHOVIES

This is a very, very generous portion for four folk, but any left over is absolutely delicious the next day with a crisp green or mixed salad.

1 shoulder of lamb, about 3½ lb (1.6 kg) on the bone

3 garlic cloves, peeled

1 x 2 oz (50 g) tin anchovies

1 whole kernel ginger preserved in syrup

12 little rosemary sprigs

2 oz (50 g) soft butter

2 tablespoons of your favourite curry paste

freshly ground black pepper

Cut the garlic in half lengthways and should there be any sign of a green shoot in the middle, remove it (it's bitter). Cut each half in half, in other words to have twelve wedges of garlic. Count out twelve anchovies as well, and cut the ginger into twelve thin slivers.

On the shoulder make 48 incisions with a sharp pointed small knife. Push garlic, anchovies, rosemary and ginger alternately into the incisions fairly evenly all over. Your index finger will make easy work of pushing the folded anchovy fillets into the holes! You could leave it now until ready to cook.

When you want to cook, pre-heat the oven to 180°C/350°F/Gas 4. Put the prepared shoulder into a roasting tray and gently rub in and over it the soft butter and the curry paste. Be very generous with pepper, then roast in the pre-heated oven for 1¼ hours. It doesn't need a gravy, as it is so moist and flavourful.

Braised Lamb Cutlets
with Garlic, Apple
and Rosemary
(page 118)
with deep-fried
noodles

Mutton Pie
with
Chestnut,
Watercress,
Apricot and Ginger
(page 114)

Roast Shoulder of Lamb
with
Garlic and Anchovies
(page 115)
and Soufflé Baked Potato
(page 138)

BRAISED LAMB CUTLETS WITH GARLIC, APPLE AND ROSEMARY

Lamb cutlets become very tender when braised, and I think they are well enhanced by the garlic and rosemary, and the bed of apples.

8 lamb cutlets on the bone, trimmed, about 3–4 oz (75–100 g) each

4 garlic cloves, peeled

8 x ½ in (1 cm) fresh rosemary sprigs

1 heaped tablespoon plain flour, seasoned with 1 teaspoon salt and 6 twirls of black pepper

4 tablespoons olive oil

1 oz (25 g) butter

4 eating apples, peeled, cored and finely sliced

600 ml (1 pint) dry white wine

Cut each prepared garlic clove into four and, making three light incisions in the trimmed cutlet, put a piece of clove into two on each cutlet and in the middle one the small sprig of fresh rosemary. Sprinkle the flour over each side of the cutlets.

In a small frying pan which will hold two cutlets, put a tablespoon of olive oil. When sizzling, add a quarter of the butter, and seal the cutlets, about 1 minute each side. There must be a sizzling sound throughout. Remove and put on kitchen paper. Adding more oil and butter each time, repeat this three more times to cook all the cutlets. Make sure the oil is hot, hot all the time. Leave to cool if you like, or continue cooking.

Pre-heat the oven to 100°C/225°F/Gas ¼.

Lightly butter a baking dish, 12 x 10 in (30 x 25 cm) approximately, and spread the prepared apples over the base. Put the prepared and part-cooked cutlets on top and pour on the wine. Cover with foil and bake in the pre-heated oven for 2 hours. Remove the foil, turn up the oven temperature to 200°C/400°F/Gas 6, and bake for a further 20 minutes.

Serve with one of the cabbage dishes (see pages 126 and 143), and Anchovy Parmesan New Potatoes (see page 134).

My Bolognese

This dish was demonstrated daily for three successive weeks prior to Christmas at the farm on my day cooking courses as a down-to-earth dish to have with bought fresh pasta when one is fed up with all the lah-di-dah food we ingest over the festive season. The reduced white wine makes all the difference, and the capers and gherkins give it a slightly sharp flavour. I served it in little cup cases made from choux pastry for lunch.

It was highly commended by all except one who, over coffee, was heard to say, 'Paying fifty quid for a day's course and he teaches us what to do with mutton mince, I ask you!'

It freezes very well, and should always be found in your freezer.

4 tablespoons olive oil

2 oz (50 g) soft butter

6 oz (175 g) onions, peeled and finely chopped

2 teaspoons garlic paste

1 lb (450 g) minced lamb

2 tablespoons tomato paste

2 tablespoons Worcestershire sauce

1 dessertspoon balsamic vinegar

salt and freshly ground black pepper

½ bottle dry white wine

8 gherkins, finely chopped

1 tablespoon drained capers

In a large frying pan heat the oil and then melt the butter. Cook the onion with the garlic paste until golden, about 6–8 minutes. Add the minced lamb along with the tomato paste, Worcestershire sauce, vinegar, and some salt and continue to cook, stirring constantly, until you are happy that all the ingredients are well 'married'. Cook on for another 30 minutes.

In a separate small saucepan heat the wine, and simmer to reduce it by half. Add to the cooked meat along with the gherkins, capers and pepper to taste.

Serve with tagliatelli, or mashed potatoes piped into a circle, or in the Choux Pastry Cups (see page 65).

Apple
Purée
(page 122)

Lamb's Liver with
Lamb's Kidneys
(page 122)
and Buttered
Caraway Cabbage
(page 143)

My
Bolognese
(page 119)

LAMB'S LIVER WITH LAMB'S KIDNEYS

For me there is nothing awful about offal, but for many people there is, so make sure, if you are cooking supper for friends, that they do not have such an aversion.

I remember going to a business lunch just as Mad Cows' Disease was the major topic. With our pre-lunch drinks the subject came up, but I had already decided to start off with brains on crostini with garlic oil and continue with sweetbreads braised in port wine. On reflection, I think I may have spoiled the others' lunch…

4 x 2 oz (50 g) slices lamb's liver

5 fl oz (150 ml) milk

4 x 2 oz (50 g) lamb's kidneys, split in two and trimmed

5 fl oz (150 ml) garlic oil

2 tablespoons plain flour

salt and freshly ground black pepper

a generous pinch of curry powder

TO SERVE

Apple Purée (opposite)

Marinate the liver in the milk and the kidneys in the garlic oil for at least 4 hours.

Pre-heat the oven to 230°C/450°F/ Gas 8.

Remove the liver from its marinade and pat dry on kitchen paper. Lightly dip in plain flour seasoned with salt, pepper and curry powder. Lay on a lightly oiled small baking tray (use some oil from the kidneys). Place the kidneys in oil in their dish alongside. Bake in the pre-heated oven for 8 minutes only.

Meanwhile warm the Apple Purée through gently. To serve, put a portion of apple on warm serving plates with the liver on top, and the drained kidney on top again.

APPLE PUREE

This is extremely simple, but it's good as a base for kidneys and liver (see left), the duck breast on page 103, and any pork dish. You could add flavourings to taste – some sage or rosemary, or a little Calvados.

The basic apple sauce can also be used in a *sweet* sense. With a little soft brown sugar and a warm spice like ground cinnamon added to taste, it can act as an apple filling for meringues, choux pastry cups, pies and pancakes, or as a sauce for many different puddings.

4 eating apples

4 oz (100 g) butter

Peel, core and thinly slice the apples. Melt the butter in a suitable saucepan then cook the apples gently until they fall. Cool a little, then liquidise and sieve.

VEGETABLE BAKE

This recipe makes a good vegetarian main-course dish, but you could also serve it in spoonfuls to accompany roast or grilled meat or chicken.

6 oz (175 g) aubergine, peeled and finely chopped

salt

2½ fl oz (75 ml) olive oil

4 oz (100 g) onions, peeled and finely chopped

5 oz (150 g) fennel bulb, finely chopped

1 red pepper, seeded and very finely chopped

a little butter for greasing the dish

6 oz (175 g) small flavourful tomatoes, thinly sliced

1–2 medium courgettes, about 6 oz (175 g), very thinly sliced

1 tablespoon chopped fresh thyme

Put the finely chopped aubergine in a large sieve, sprinkle with salt and leave to drain for 1 hour. Rinse briefly to get rid of the sour juices, then pat dry on kitchen paper.

In a frying pan heat 1 tablespoon of the olive oil and cook the onion, fennel and aubergine until golden. (If you like garlic, a crushed clove added at this stage would add oomph to the dish.) Add the red pepper and continue cooking for 10 minutes.

Lightly butter the base and sides of a suitably sized cooking dish (it should be quite deep), and spread the cooked mixture on the base. Spread over this, alternately, side by side and slightly overlapping, the tomato and courgette. Pour over the remaining olive oil and scatter with the chopped fresh thyme. You can leave it now for a while.

When you wish to cook, pre-heat the oven to 200°C/400°F/Gas 6, and bake for 45 minutes. You can, if you wish, add finely grated fresh Parmesan cheese to the top at this stage and flash the dish under a hot grill. A tablespoon of freshly chopped parsley sprinkled on provides additional flavour.

Baked
Cabbage
Pizzas
(page 126)

Vegetable
Bake
(page 123)

Leek
with
Tarragon
and
Cheese
(page 147)

BAKED CABBAGE PIZZAS

Recently an unexpected extra guest turned up at the farm. The two people with whom she was staying both thought the other had phoned to ask if she could come along. No problem, thought I, simply lay another place at the table, and give everybody a smaller piece of quiche. The pre-dinner glasses of wine were duly poured and offered. It was only when I produced the canapés – amongst which were mini sausage rolls – that the 'intruder' announced that not only was she a vegetarian but she was also on a gluten-free diet!

Necessity being the mother of invention, after taking an enormous swig from my glass and giving a theatrical smile, I rushed over to my neighbours', begged a cabbage from their garden, and produced the following alternative main course.

1 firm Savoy cabbage

5 tablespoons oil of choice

sea salt and freshly ground black pepper

8 oz (225 g) Roquefort cheese, crumbled

TO SERVE

Tomato Sauce (see page 39)

chopped fresh chives and/or parsley

Pre-heat the oven to 180°C/350°F/Gas 4.

Lay your cabbage on its side and cut four slices crossways through the middle, each about ¾ in (2 cm) thick. Do not, at this stage, remove the outer leaves, as these tend to fall away during the cooking. Lightly oil a baking tray with 1 tablespoon of oil, and place the four rounds of cabbage on top. Pour 1 tablespoon of oil over each round and season with black pepper and sea salt. Bake in the pre-heated oven for 20 minutes if, like me, you prefer crisp veggies, or slightly longer if you have trouble with your teeth!

Pre-heat the grill. Warm through the Tomato Sauce in a small pan.

When the cabbage pizzas are cooked, remove from the oven and sprinkle 2 oz (50 g) of the crumbled Roquefort cheese on to each. Grill approximately 3 in (7.5 cm) from the heat for 2 minutes until nice and bubbling. Transfer to your plates, spoon a quarter of the warmed Tomato Sauce on to each, and serve straightaway. Chopped chives and parsley sprinkled over the top make a nice presentation.

You could make mini 'pizzas', which are delicious served with steaks. From larger cabbage slices, you could cut small circles using a biscuit or scone cutter. Cook in the same way as above. (Use the leftover cabbage in a sliced cabbage recipe, see page 143.)

SIMPLY
Splendid
VEGETABLE
ACCOMPANIMENTS

Buttered
Caraway
Cabbage
(page 143)

Baked
Potato
Circles
(page 134)

Balsamic
Onions
(page 130)

BALSAMIC ONIONS

I have been using balsamic vinegar for many years, but of late it has become so fashionable and trendy I wonder how production plants in Italy cope – a bit like my Sancerre theory of some years ago, when Sancerre became available *everywhere*, but this huge quantity of wine was supposed to emanate from just one small valley…

These onions are a bit like onion marmalade, but with that unique, balsamic flavour. They go well with steaks, liver and kidneys, and the duck breast (see pages 111, 122 and 103).

2 large onions, about 6 oz (175 g) each

2 tablespoons garlic oil

1 dessertspoon soft brown sugar

1 tablespoon balsamic vinegar

Put each onion one by one down on your work surface with the stalk to the left and, as close as you can to this, insert a kitchen fork to keep the onion steady. Using a sharp serrated carving knife slice off extremely thin slices with the skin on. It is a relatively simple job then to remove the thin pieces of skin. Chop the circles in half.

In a large frying pan heat the oil and add the onions. Cook for about 15 minutes, stirring from time to time with a wooden spoon. Add the brown sugar and the balsamic vinegar, and cook for a further 2 minutes. They can be left for a few hours, or overnight, at this stage.

When you wish to serve, the onions take about 3–4 minutes to heat through.

DEEP-FRIED PICKLING ONIONS

When pickling onions are on the scene, I always pickle about ten 1 lb (450 g) jars' worth, and devour them weeks before they are properly ready. I still haven't come across a commercial recipe that resembles the one I use, but whenever I see a WI stall or farmyard stall selling them, I buy two or three jars.

But when I get my first lot of pickling onions, I always make this simple dish to start off with. It's wonderful with steak or any plain grilled meat.

24 pickling onions, about 12 oz (350 g) in weight

oil for deep-frying

1 tablespoon red wine vinegar or raspberry vinegar

Peel, top and tail the onions. Heat your deep-fryer to 180°C/350°F and simply cook the onions for 3 minutes only. Turn out on to kitchen paper to drain, then place in a serving dish. Cover with the chosen vinegar.

BAKED GARLIC CORIANDER SHALLOTS

Shallots are subtler in flavour than onions, and they are wonderfully enhanced by the garlic, coriander and raspberry vinegar.

10 oz (300 g) shallots, about 28 in all, peeled

1 tablespoon whole coriander seeds, lightly crushed

10 fl oz (300 ml) garlic oil

2 tablespoons raspberry vinegar

Pre-heat the oven to 200°C/400°F/Gas 6.

Place the shallots in a dish that will hold them in one layer, sprinkle with the coriander seeds and pour in the garlic oil. Cook for 20 minutes in the pre-heated oven, making sure you stir the shallots after 10 and 15 minutes. Remove from the oven and leave.

When you wish to serve, strain the shallots, retaining the oil. Put the shallots back into the dish with only 2 table-spoons of the oil, plus the vinegar. Heat through in the oven at the same temperature as above for 5 minutes.

Deep-fried
Pickling
Onions
(page 131)

Asparagus
Parcels
(page 143)

Anchovy
Parmesan
New Potatoes
(page 134)

ANCHOVY PARMESAN NEW POTATOES

The following paste is very easily made, and the quantities are probably too much for potatoes for four folk. It stores very well, though, in the fridge in a screw-top jar, is delicious with other vegetables, and also melts well over pasta.

1 lb (450 g) small new potatoes, washed

salt

ANCHOVY AND PARMESAN PASTE

6 anchovies

4 oz (100 g) Parmesan cheese, finely grated

4 tablespoons olive oil

1 oz (25 g) soft butter

Make the paste first. Simply put all the ingredients in a food processor and process to a paste. Decant into a screw-top jar and chill if making well in advance.

When ready to serve, put the potatoes in a pan of boiling seasoned water and cook until tender, about 15 minutes. Strain and return to the pan. Toss in some of the anchovy and Parmesan paste, using as much or as little as you like.

BAKED POTATO CIRCLES

These make rather a splendid potato accompaniment to a number of dishes, but if you make them thin enough you could serve something different, even a fried egg, on top!

10 oz (300 g) King Edward potatoes, peeled

1¼ oz (30 g) salted butter, melted

Pre-heat the oven to 200°C/400°F/Gas 6.

Slice the potatoes very, very thinly, and divide them into four equal portions. Lightly grease a baking tray with a little of the butter. Start by putting one slice of potato from one pile in one quarter of the tray and then build up around it a circle, overlapping the slices as if they were tiles on a roof. Repeat three more times to make four tiered potato circles in all. Paint with melted butter and bake in the pre-heated oven for 20–25 minutes. Remove from the baking tray to hot serving plates using a fish slice.

CURRIED CUBED POTATOES

These are tasty and moreish, very good with pork or lamb, beef or chicken – anything, in fact!

1¼ lb (550 g) King Edward potatoes, peeled

salt and freshly ground black pepper

6 oz (175 g) beef dripping

1 heaped dessertspoon curry paste

Cut the potatoes into 1 in (2.5 cm) cubes, then boil in salted water until just starting to cook. Strain, then shake in the pan to get the sides of the cubes slightly floury.

Pre-heat the oven to 200°C/400°F/ Gas 6, and put the beef dripping in a roasting tray to melt. Put your hob on to high as well.

When the dripping is really hot, take the roasting tray out of the oven and put on to the hot hob. Throw in the partly cooked potato cubes and you should get a wonderful hissing sound like in a fish and chip shop when they pour the chips into the boiling oil. Cook for 30 minutes in the pre-heated oven, then remove and strain off the dripping. Return the drained potato cubes to the oven for a further 15 minutes.

Just prior to serving, stir in the curry paste so that all the cubes are coated. Serve immediately.

Soufflé
Baked
Potatoes
(page 138)

Garlic
Puréed
Potatoes
(page 139)

SOUFFLE BAKED POTATOES

These can be served as a simple supper by themselves, or as an accompaniment to a plainly cooked piece of meat, chicken or fish.

4 potatoes, at least 8 oz (225 g) each in weight

salt and freshly ground black pepper

4 oz (100 g) cottage or curd cheese

1–2 tablespoons grated Parmesan cheese

2 teaspoons coarse-grain mustard

2 small eggs, separated

Pre-heat the oven to 220°C/425°F/Gas 7. Wrap the potatoes in foil and cook for 1¼ hours. Unwrap and cool a little. Reduce the temperature of the oven to 190°C/375°F/Gas 5.

Take a slice lengthwise off the top of each potato, not just a small lid. Scoop the flesh of each out into a bowl, leaving a good shell. Don't forget to scrape the flesh from the top slice as well.

Mash the potato flesh well, then mix in seasoning to taste, the cottage or curd cheese, half the Parmesan, the mustard and the egg yolks. Whisk the egg whites until stiff in a separate bowl, and fold lightly into the mixture. Spoon back into the potato shells. Sprinkle with the remaining Parmesan and bake in the pre-heated oven for a further 15–20 minutes until the potatoes puff up and turn golden. Eat immediately.

GARLIC PUREED POTATOES

When we were cooking in South Africa recently, we served these potatoes to accompany a variation of the cubed salmon dish on page 82. As it is extremely difficult in Johannesburg to get really fresh fish, but easy to obtain locally farmed trout, the latter was used. We coated it with chopped pistachio nuts, breadcrumbs, cheese and herbs, pan-fried it for a few minutes to give it a barbecued look, then finished it off in a very hot oven. The potatoes got as many admiring comments as the fish.

2 lb (900 g) King Edward potatoes, peeled

salt

2 tablespoons garlic oil

4 oz (100 g) butter, melted

1 teaspoon garlic paste

Cut the potatoes evenly, then cook until soft in boiling salted water. Drain, then put into the food processor and add the garlic oil, butter and garlic paste. Process at a high speed to a purée, then pass through a coarse sieve. When needed, re-heat in a double saucepan.

A lovely variation is to then stir in 1 tablespoon of very finely diced sun-dried tomatoes and the chopped green ends of spring onions.

FRIED SLICED GARLIC POTATOES

Nursery fodder – like upmarket chips – but this is a dish I love to prepare when I'm using up a cold roast or feeling particularly self-indulgent. Enhance it with a smattering of chopped fresh herbs.

1 lb (450 g) clean new potatoes

salt

4 tablespoons garlic oil

Put the potatoes into boiling salted water, bring back to the boil, and cook for 4 minutes only. Strain and leave to cool, then slice in circles.

When you wish to cook, put the oil in your frying pan. When hot, add the potato slices and, using a wooden spatula, pan-fry, turning, for 10–12 minutes. Remove using a slotted spoon and sprinkle with sea salt.

Some people prefer these potatoes done very well like chips. Carry on cooking until you get this effect.

Baked
Garlic
Coriander
Shallots
(page 131)

Curried
Cubed
Potatoes
(page 135)

Vegetable
Spaghetti
(page 142)

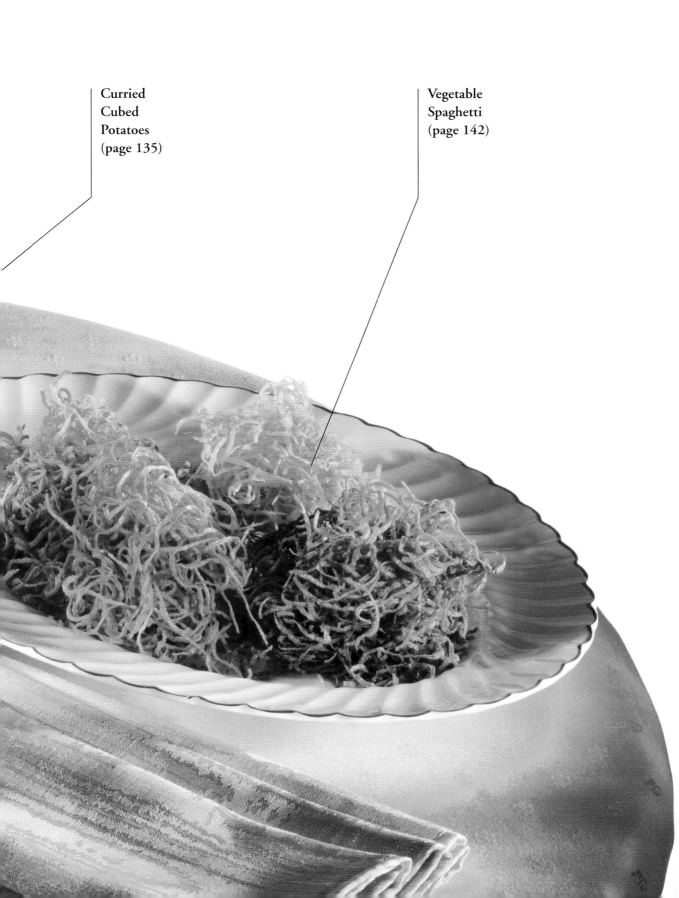

VEGETABLE SPAGHETTI

Some time ago we discovered a wonderful, but simple, piece of equipment which Lakeland Plastics sell at their numerous outlets and through their mail-order service. It is a small machine called a *Saladacco*, and it gives you endless strips of vegetable 'spaghetti' or *thin*, thin rounds of root vegetables. It is versatile, easy to use and takes up little space in your cupboard.

When either lightly boiled or deep-fried the spaghetti-like veg are a talking point and are always tasty. The spaghetti or circles are splendid served as side dishes with steaks, fish, pâtés, etc.

Using this machine and your deep-fryer, for four people you need 6 oz (175 g) of turnip or any other root vegetable (potato, carrot, celeriac, parsnip, swede). Peel the veg and cut a flat surface on one side. Attach this to the cutting edge inside the machine and then put on the lid. Quickly turn the handle, and the vegetable will turn into spaghetti or circles, depending on which cutter you choose to use.

Heat your oil to 180°C/350°F and when it has reached this temperature put the prepared vegetables into a large metal sieve and submerge in the hot fat. They will be ready in only 2–3 minutes.

If you lack this crafty machine, you can use a sharp potato peeler. Shave off very thin slices of root veg. About 4 oz (100 g) of these will take only 3 minutes to cook through at the same temperature as above.

ASPARAGUS PARCELS

You can occasionally find these cigarette-thin asparagus spears in supermarkets or street markets. They can be local – the best coming from Suffolk or the Southport area – or from much further afield. You can serve the parcels hot with melted butter as an accompaniment to steak or chicken, or cold with mayonnaise as a garnish for salmon or other fish dishes or the Potted Prawns on page 27.

20 cigarette-thin asparagus spears, about 4 oz (100 g), trimmed (see page 54)

1 leek leaf

salt

Cut the leek leaf into 8 in (20 cm) long strips, ¼ in (5 mm) thick, and blanch in boiling salted water for 1 minute. Strain and refresh under running cold water.

Take 5 asparagus spears at a time and use one strip of leek to tie them into parcels. (This does get easier after the first attempt!) Steam for 5 minutes over salted boiling water. Serve hot or leave to go cold.

BUTTERED CARAWAY CABBAGE

A fresh firm white cabbage is needed for this dish which from start to finish takes about 10 minutes only. It makes a lovely accompaniment to the Tropical Chicken Stir-fry on page 98 or the Battered Monkfish on page 95.

12 oz (350 g) cabbage (not the stalks), finely shredded

4 tablespoons oil of choice

1 oz (25 g) soft butter

½ teaspoon garlic paste

5 fl oz (150 ml) dry cider

1 teaspoon caraway seeds

salt and freshly ground black pepper

Heat the oil until smoking in a suitable pan, and then add and melt in the butter. Stir in the garlic paste then chuck in the prepared cabbage. Stir-fry for 5 minutes, before adding the cider and caraway seeds. Stir-fry for 2 more minutes, then sprinkle with salt and pepper and serve.

Marinated
Brussels Sprouts
with
Poppy and
Sesame Seeds
(page 146)

Purée
of
Celeriac
(page 146)

Fried
Sliced
Garlic
Potatoes
(page 139)

MARINATED BRUSSELS SPROUTS WITH POPPY AND SESAME SEEDS

The first time new season sprouts appear in the kitchen (they are definitely better after the first really cold night), I always, but always cook them unadulterated in boiling salted water and serve them *al dente*. As the weeks go by they are garnished with fresh chestnuts, with bacon bits, twirls of lemon, etc., and after Christmas, when they are OK but nothing to write home about, this is how I cook them. The wine you choose will dictate the outcome: sweet or dry according to your own palate. Serve them with steak, roast beef or chicken breast dishes.

8 oz (225 g) Brussels sprouts

2 tablespoons white wine of choice

1 tablespoon freshly squeezed lemon juice

2 tablespoons garlic oil

1 level teaspoon garlic paste

1 level dessertspoon each of poppy and sesame seeds

Remove the outer leaves and the hard stalk from the sprouts. Turn each sprout on to its side and cut into ⅛ in (3 mm) circles. Toss these circles in the wine of your choice along with the lemon juice, then leave to marinate for about 30 minutes.

When ready to serve, warm up the garlic oil in a frying pan with the garlic paste. Drain the sprouts, retaining the wine, and then add to the pan along with the seeds. Toss together, then stir for 3 minutes. Add the wine and cook for a further minute. Serve at once.

PUREE OF CELERIAC

This purée makes a particularly good bed for the Marinated Cubed Salmon on page 82. If using as a vegetable accompaniment for something else, you could sprinkle with toasted pine kernels or desiccated coconut. Other root vegetables can be puréed in the same way.

1 lb (450 g) celeriac, weighed after peeling

salt and freshly ground black pepper

5 fl oz (150 ml) double cream, fromage frais or crème fraîche

Cut the celeriac into ¼ in (5 mm) cubes and boil in lightly salted water until quite soft, about 6 minutes. Drain well and dry on kitchen paper.

In a food processor blend with the cream. Season to taste with salt and pepper. If preparing in advance, re-heat in a double saucepan.

LEEK WITH TARRAGON AND CHEESE

Leeks, members of the onion family, can be exciting or boring. This recipe combines *two* different treatments of leek, and I think it's delicious!

1 lb (450 g) leeks

1 tablespoon olive oil

6 oz (175 g) full-fat cream cheese

1 oz (25 g) fresh tarragon, finely chopped

salt and freshly ground black pepper

DEEP-FRIED LEEK JULIENNE

1 large leek

oil of choice for deep-frying

Prepare the deep-fried julienne of leek first. Top and tail the leek, then cut it into 3 in (7.5 cm) sections and then cut these in half through the length to give semi-circle sections, 3 in (7.5 cm) long. From each section remove the inner part and put to one side. With a sharp knife make very fine cuts lengthways to give long thin strands, and then do exactly the same with the inner pieces removed earlier.

Wash the prepared leek shreds, and dry well on kitchen paper. Heat the oil for deep-frying to 180°C/350°F, then deep-fry the leek for 1–2 minutes until golden brown. Drain well on kitchen paper and leave to cool. When cool, the leeks will become crisp. This can be done in the morning or the night before (store in an airtight container).

Prepare the remainder of the leeks just before serving. Top and tail them, then cut in half lengthways. Cut each half into quarters to give long thin strips. Then cut across the strips at ¼ in (5 mm) intervals to give finely diced leeks.

Heat the olive oil in a suitable pan, and add the finely diced leek. Cook until tender on a gentle heat, about 5–10 minutes. Add the cream cheese, tarragon, salt and pepper, and stir until the cheese melts and coats the leeks. Serve immediately, sprinkled with the deep-fried julienne of leek.

SIMPLY
Splendid
DESSERTS

CAPE BRANDY TART

A 'dish' tart rather than one made in pastry. The nuts, glacé fruit and booze (especially if you use Cape Velvet, the South African version of Bailey's) give it an exotic feel. Make it the day before, then reheat at the last moment.

2 oz (50 g) soft butter

4 oz (100 g) soft brown sugar

1 large egg, lightly beaten

2½ oz (65 g) self-raising flour

2 oz (50 g) shelled pecan nuts, chopped

3 oz (75 g) good quality glacé fruits, finely chopped

½ level teaspoon bicarbonate of soda

2½ fl oz (75 ml) booze of choice (cooking brandy or Cape Velvet)

2½ fl oz (75 ml) boiling water

SAUCE TOPPING

2 oz (50 g) soft brown sugar

5 fl oz (150 ml) booze of choice (as above)

Pre-heat the oven to 180°C/350°F/Gas 4.

Cream the butter and sugar together then slowly beat in the egg. Fold in the remaining dry ingredients, and then stir in the booze and boiling water. Pour into an oval dish of about 7 x 5 in (18 x 13 cm) and 3 in (7.5 cm) deep, and bake in the pre-heated oven for 1½ hours.

Meanwhile, melt the sauce brown sugar with the chosen booze. As the tart is cooling, pour this mixture over it and leave to soak in. At this stage you should leave the tart overnight. To serve, reheat in the oven at the same temperature as above, for 30 minutes, and serve with cream.

ALMOND SAUTERNES CAKES

You could serve these cakes as a pudding, or at tea-time, split in half horizontally, filled with sweetened whipped cream and scattered with strawberry slices or other summer fruit. They're delicious, too, used as the sponge in a trifle (see the recipe opposite).

6 medium eggs, separated

6 oz (175 g) caster sugar

finely grated rind of 1 orange

5 fl oz (150 ml) Sauternes or other sweet white wine

4 oz (100 g) ground almonds

4 oz (100 g) plain white flour

Pre-heat the oven to 180°C/350°F/Gas 4, and line two 10 in (25 cm) round spring-sided cake tins with good greaseproof paper.

In a warm mixer bowl, beat the egg yolks using an electric whisk. When creamy, slowly and gradually beat in 4 oz (100 g) of the sugar. Beat in the orange rind and wine, then fold in the ground almonds and flour.

In a separate clean bowl whisk the egg whites until stiff, beating in the remaining sugar. Fold this into the egg yolk mix, then pour into the prepared cake tins. Bake in the pre-heated oven for 15 minutes. Turn the oven temperature down to 150°C/300°F/Gas 2, and cook for a further 15 minutes. Cool on a cooling tray.

COWBOY TRIFLE

Some time ago some friends kindly gave me the loan of their beach house for three days. This was situated literally on the shores of Table Bay in Cape Town, and it was simply magnificent. I went to sleep with the sounds of the waves churning at the bottom of the garden, and woke up to bright clear blue skies with the whole outline of Table Mountain on the horizon. I decided late on the Friday to have a lunch party on the Saturday, and managed to gather some fourteen friends together. I had taken out with me a side of smoked salmon, eggs were in abundance, and the Bolognese on page 119 took no time to do using a small roasting tin instead of a frying pan. I also knew of an excellent shop in Newlands that sold freshly made pasta. Unfortunately, though, other shops were some distance away and as I had tickets for the ballet on the Friday night, I was left with very little time to get my act together.

One of my friends suggested I make my trifle for a pud, and I said, 'No way do I have time to make sponges and fresh custard, we'll have to buy some Cape cheeses and give them that with masses of fresh seasonal fruit.' We literally raced round the Pick-and-Pay supermarket, and when we got back to the ranch, so to speak, I discovered that we had acquired bought ready-made sponges, a bottle of peach schnapps (cheap to buy, and much more interesting than the conventional sherry), and, believe it or not, a carton of freshly made vanilla custard. I did do my trifle, therefore, and it went down well.

1 Almond Sauternes Cake (see opposite), or bought sponge

15 fl oz (450 ml) peach schnapps

4 satsumas, peeled and segmented

1 lb (450 g) tin apricots, strained and then liquidised

10 fl oz (300 ml) double cream

2 tablespoons icing sugar

10 fl oz (300 ml) bought vanilla custard (or home-made, see page 187)

4 oz (100 g) good chocolate (I used Toblerone), coarsely grated

Spilt your cake in half horizontally. Put one circle on the base of your round serving dish and pour on 5 fl oz (150 ml) of the peach schnapps. Spread on this, in ever-decreasing circles, the prepared satsuma segments, and over this spread the puréed apricots.

Whip the cream with the icing sugar, then spread half of this on top of the apricots, followed by the other round of sponge. Pour on the balance of the schnapps, and leave to soak through, covered with cling film.

Pour over the vanilla custard, and pipe the balance of the double cream in stars round the edge. Sprinkle the chocolate on the top.

Almond
Sauternes
Cake
(page 150)

Cowboy
Trifle
(page 151)

Cape
Brandy
Tart
(page 149)

TANGY LEMON CREAMS

I use the measured ½ oz (15 g) sachets of powdered gelatine, as I find it virtually impossible to use the leaf stuff. And although the recipes in this book are mainly for four people, this mixture will fill *six* hock glasses! Make the cream in the morning, or at least a few hours in advance to allow them to set.

5 fl oz (150 ml) dry white wine of choice
(a Sauvignon Blanc from the New World
would be ideal)

½ oz (15 g) powdered gelatine

3 medium eggs, separated

4 oz (100 g) caster sugar

3 lemons

10 fl oz (300 ml) double cream,
lightly beaten

Pour the wine into a small pan and sprinkle on the gelatine. Shake gently and leave to one side in a cool place.

In a warm bowl beat the egg yolks until light and fluffy, at least 8 minutes, using an electric whisk, and then add the caster sugar little by little, continuing to beat until the sugar is all absorbed. The yolks and sugar must be thick enough so that a ribbon-like trail formed by the whisk stays on the surface, and doesn't immediately sink back into the mixture.

In another small pan gently heat the juice from the *three* lemons along with the finely grated rind of *one*. Dribble this slowly over the egg yolk mix whilst continuing to beat at a high speed. Fold in the lightly beaten cream.

In a clean glass or metal bowl, and using an electric whisk, beat the egg whites to stiff, certainly not floppy, peaks. Fold into the cream mix.

Whilst the egg whites are being beaten, put the gelatine on to the lowest heat possible and dissolve. Pour through a heated fine metal sieve into the mix, and fold together carefully. Spoon into your glasses, and leave to chill.

RICH CHOCOLATE CREAM WITH MASCARPONE

Having made a small batch of meringue nests for a friend's kid's birthday party, I was faced with four left-over egg yolks. Being a chocoholic, I made the following dish on the spur of the moment, in the hope that it would turn out OK. The next night I had close friends round for supper and I offered this as well as two other puddings. They all went for the chocolate, and their initial remark as they sucked and swallowed the first teaspoon was, 'Oh, it's so *rich*!…' But they finished it all, leaving extremely clean ramekins, and even went on to sample one or two of the other puds.

The success of the dish relies on the quality of the chocolate you use, however. Look at the ingredients list on the packets – which can be quite daunting, I know – and choose the chocolate with the highest amount of cocoa butter or cocoa solids. I always buy Menier Chocolat Pâtissier, a dark chocolate, when cooking at the farm.

4 egg yolks

6 oz (175 g) good dark chocolate, chopped

4 tablespoons Frangelico (a hazelnut liqueur)

2 oz (50 g) butter

TO SERVE

4 oz (100 g) Mascarpone cheese

In a heatproof bowl over simmering water beat together all the ingredients until the chocolate has melted. Beat for a further 30 seconds, then pour into four 3 in (7.5 cm) ramekins. The portion may look mean, but it's not, as it is very rich. Leave to set in the fridge.

Top with the Mascarpone cheese before serving. Pipe or spread all over.

Rich Chocolate
Cream with
Mascarpone
(page 155)

Earl Grey
Crème
Brûlée
(page 158)

Tangy
Lemon Creams
(page 154)
and small
Spiced Biscuits
(page 183)

EARL GREY CREME BRULEE

This isn't at all a traditional 'burnt cream', but the top is crunchy, and the custard beneath rich and thick, with a very unusual flavour.

10 fl oz (300 ml) double cream

4 teaspoons Earl Grey tea

2 egg yolks

1 level tablespoon caster sugar

½ teaspoon vanilla extract

TOPPING

about 4 tablespoons demerara sugar

Pre-heat the oven to 140°C/275°F/Gas 1.

Bring the cream and tea to the boil together in a saucepan. Remove from the heat and leave to infuse for a further 10 minutes. Strain well.

Beat the egg yolks with the sugar until quite pale in colour and heavy in texture, using an electric whisk, about 4-5 minutes. Pour the cooled cream into them through a fine sieve, and mix in well, together with the vanilla.

Divide the custard between four 3 in (7.5 cm) ramekins. Place the ramekins in a bain-marie, with enough hot water to come half-way up their sides. Bake in the pre-heated oven for 15 minutes until lightly set. Remove from the oven, and allow to cool.

Meanwhile pre-heat the grill to very hot.

Line a flat baking tray with a double thickness of foil, matt side up. Sprinkle the sugar on in four circles that will fit the ramekins. Grill until caramelised, then leave to set. Simply transfer when cool, using a palette knife, to the tops of the custards.

PAVLOVA ROLL

When testing this recipe, I was reminded of a wine educational trip to New Zealand eight years ago. Practically everywhere I went the 'national dish', pavlova, was served as a pudding, and before you had digested the first mouthful, the hostess would invariably ask, 'And what do you think of *my* pavlova?' Virtually every family seemingly had their own interpretation of the dish. It became quite difficult…

When I was actually demonstrating this pavlova roll on one of the day courses at the farm, an otherwise keen-to-learn cook said, as I was spreading the mixture into the prepared tin: 'Can't see that working. I always use Delia's recipe, and she doesn't go in for that cornflour and vinegar nonsense.' Well, it does work, and although I tried to get her to sample mine, she politely declined!

3 medium egg whites

6 oz (175 g) caster sugar

3 teaspoons cornflour

1 teaspoon white wine vinegar

a generous splash of vanilla extract

FILLING

10 fl oz (300 ml) double cream

2 tablespoons caster sugar

2 tablespoons good glacé fruits, finely chopped

icing sugar

Pre-heat the oven to 140°C/275°F/Gas 1, and line a baking tin measuring about 11 x 9 in (28 x 23 cm) with good greaseproof paper.

In a cold mixing bowl, using an electric whisk, beat the egg whites until stiff and more than quadrupled in size, then slowly and gradually add the sugar, beating continually until all the sugar is in. Beat in the cornflour, vinegar and vanilla extract. Spread the mixture evenly and gently into the prepared tin, using a palette knife. Bake in the pre-heated oven for 30 minutes.

Remove from the oven, cover with a slightly damp tea towel and leave until cold. Fill and roll when cold. Turn out of the tin on to a piece of silicone paper liberally sprinkled with icing sugar. Whip the cream until stiff with the sugar, then fold in the fruits. Spread over the top of the pavlova, then roll it up carefully. Dust with icing sugar and serve fairly swiftly.

Baked
Curried
Cream
Pineapple
Meringue
(page 163)

Pavlova
Roll
(page 159)

Meringue
Hearts
with
Coeurs à la Crème
(page 162)

MERINGUE HEARTS WITH COEURS A LA CREME

These heart-shaped puds are lovely served with a purée of strawberries or raspberries (see page 179). Start the preparation at least the day before. The meringues keep well in an airtight tin, and the coeurs à la crème need to be done the day before.

2 medium egg whites

4 oz (100 g) caster sugar

COEURS A LA CREME

a little oil for greasing the moulds

10 fl oz (300 ml) double cream

1 heaped tablespoon caster sugar

½ teaspoon vanilla extract

8 oz (225 g) cream cheese (low- or full-fat)

2 medium egg whites

Pre-heat the oven to 100°C/200°F/the very lowest gas possible. Oil four coeur à la crème moulds and line them thereafter with butter muslin. Draw the outline of the heart-shaped moulds eight times on good greaseproof or Bakewell paper and place on baking trays.

To make the meringue hearts, whip the egg whites, using an electric whisk, until soft peaks (still a bit floppy), then start adding the sugar a tablespoon at a time until three-quarters has been beaten in. Fold in the remainder when the whites are stiff and glossy. Pipe on to the eight pencilled heart outlines then bake in the pre-heated oven for 1¾ hours. Leave in the turned-off oven until really cold.

To make the coeurs à la crème, beat the double cream with the sugar and vanilla extract until quite thick, then fold in the cream cheese. Beat the egg whites in a separate bowl until stiff and firm, using an electric whisk, then fold into the cream cheese mix. Divide between the four moulds and leave on a plastic tray, covered with cling film, overnight in the fridge.

When you wish to serve, simply put four meringue hearts out on to your individual plates. Place a turned-out crème on top of each, then top with the remaining four meringue hearts.

BAKED CURRIED CREAM PINEAPPLE MERINGUE

This is an unusually flavoured mini version of Baked Alaska. It takes no time to do, so long as you are well prepared, with a certain amount done the night before.

4 dessertspoons double cream

2 teaspoons soft brown sugar

1 teaspoon curry paste of choice

4 x ½ in (1 cm) thick fresh pineapple rings

a little butter for greasing the tray

4 tablespoons rum

MERINGUE MIX

2 medium egg whites

4 oz (100 g) caster sugar

The day before, mix the cream, sugar and curry paste together. Divide between four tiny jam tart tins, and freeze. Prepare the four pineapple rings, and cut the circle in the middle to the same size as the jam tart tins. Put on a lightly buttered tray and pour a tablespoon of rum over each. Cover with cling film and leave for at least 4 hours.

When you wish to serve, pre-heat the oven to 190°C/375°F/Gas 5. Make a stiff meringue mixture from the egg whites and caster sugar (see opposite for the method). Put into a piping bag with a star nozzle.

Put the frozen round of cream in the middle of each pineapple ring. Pipe on the meringue mix to completely cover each pineapple ring and bake in the pre-heated oven for 10 minutes until golden. Transfer to individual plates using a fish slice, and eat hot.

Sweet
Pear
Bake
(page 166)

Malva
Pudding
(page 168)

Brown
Betty
Apples
(page 166)

SWEET PEAR BAKE

This is a satisfying and delicious pud which is ideal for cold evenings. It can be prepared well in advance and then baked at the last moment.

2 lb (900 g) ripe pears

4 tablespoons peach schnapps

2 oz (50 g) soft brown sugar

6 oz (175 g) chocolate digestive biscuits, liquidised

1 teaspoon vanilla extract

2 oz (50 g) nibbed almonds

2 oz (50 g) soft butter

TO SERVE

crème fraîche

Peel, quarter and core the pears, and put them in a bowl. Cover with the peach schnapps and leave to marinate for at least 4 hours.

Mix the sugar, liquidised biscuits, vanilla and almonds together with the runny butter.

In a 10 in (25 cm) round baking dish, spread the pears, and dab the other mixture over the top. Put in the fridge until required.

When ready to cook, pre-heat the oven to 180°C/350°F/Gas 4. Bake the pudding in the pre-heated oven for 1 hour. Serve warm with *crème fraîche*.

BROWN BETTY APPLES

One of the most popular autumnal puds at Miller Howe is our apple charlotte. I've made this for years, and usually serve it with a separate hot custard. Trying to have as much preparation done ahead of time in this book, I did a few experiments with the following dish, a variant of the charlotte. As you will observe, it can now be prepared and cooked in the morning, turned out when cold on to a baking tray, and then literally finished off whilst you are having the main course.

You need four ramekins, 3–3¾ in (7–9 cm) in diameter.

a little butter for greasing the ramekins

4 Savoury Croûtons (see page 64), to fit the base of the ramekins

2 eating apples, about 5 oz (150 g) each, peeled, cored and quartered

10 fl oz (300 ml) cider of choice

2 oz (50 g) soft brown sugar

2 oz (50 g) brown breadcrumbs

CUSTARD CREAM

5 fl oz (150 ml) double cream

1 egg

1 egg yolk

½ nutmeg, freshly grated

1 oz (25 g) brown flour

1 oz (25 g) soft brown sugar

TO SERVE

4 tablespoons fromage frais

Pre-heat the oven to 190°C/375°F/Gas 5. Lightly grease your ramekins and line the base and sides with cooking cling film, leaving some overlapping. Put a croûton in the base of each ramekin.

Cut each quarter of apple into fine slices – about eight to a quarter! – and leave to marinate in the cider for about 15 minutes. Drain the cider and keep to one side.

Mix the brown sugar and breadcrumbs together in a bowl. Put a fanned quarter of apple slices on to each croûton in the ramekins, and cover with some of the breadcrumbs and sugar mix.

In a separate bowl, mix the cream, egg and egg yolk, nutmeg, brown flour and sugar together to a custard-like cream.

Spoon one-eighth of this over each prepared dish, then add the rest of the apples, finishing off with the balance of the custard cream. Top with the balance of the crumb mixture.

Bake in the pre-heated oven for 20 minutes in a bain-marie filled with enough hot water to come half-way up the sides of the ramekins.

In the meantime, put the retained cider into a saucepan and simmer down to about 2 tablespoons. This will take approximately 10 minutes.

Remove the cooked puds from the oven and when cool, remove from the ramekins (this is where the cling film helps). Put back on to a lightly greased baking tray, and keep until needed.

When you wish to serve, pre-heat the oven to 230°C/450°F/Gas 8. Put ½ tablespoon of reduced cider over each and bake for 8 minutes. Serve immediately with *fromage frais.*

MALVA PUDDING

I've been demonstrating this new pudding on my day course at the farm, and although it looks very unpromising – definitely an old-fashioned, spongey, sticky, steamed pudding type of thing – it's been very warmly received indeed. We doubled the recipe for the ladies, and there was never any left from the huge dish we used! If you do have leftovers, they re-heat very successfully in a warm oven.

8 oz (225 g) caster sugar

1 medium egg

1 tablespoon apricot jam

7½ fl oz (225 ml) milk

4 oz (100 g) plain flour, sieved

1 teaspoon bicarbonate of soda

a tiny pinch of salt

1 tablespoon warm melted butter

½ teaspoon malt vinegar

SAUCE TOPPING

2½ oz (65 g) butter

2½ oz (65 g) caster sugar

5 fl oz (150 ml) booze of choice (cooking brandy or Bailey's)

2½ fl oz (75 ml) double cream

TO SERVE

whipped double cream

Pre-heat the oven to 180°C/350°F/Gas 4, and lightly butter an ovenproof dish approximately 7 x 5 in (18 x 13 cm) in diameter, and 2 in (5 cm) deep.

Whisk the sugar, egg and apricot jam together in a warmed bowl until light and fluffy. Slowly pour on the milk, beating all the time, then fold in the sieved plain flour, bicarbonate of soda and salt. When well mixed, add the warm melted butter and vinegar. Pour into the prepared dish, cover with foil and bake in the pre-heated oven for 1¼ hours.

Meanwhile make the sauce topping. Mix the ingredients in a small pan, and melt gently together. Bring to simmering point, and pour over the pudding when it is cooked. Leave to soak in for about 10 minutes before serving, with whipped cream.

CHESTNUT ROULADE

Roulades are light, good to eat and good to look at. The chestnut purée gives this one an inimitable flavour.

a little oil for greasing the tin

5 oz (150 g) tinned natural chestnut purée

3 tablespoons cooking brandy

5 medium eggs, separated

5 oz (150 g) caster sugar

FILLING

icing sugar

10 fl oz (300 ml) double cream, whipped

2 tablespoons rum

Pre-heat the oven to 180°C/350°F/Gas 4, and line an 11 x 8 in (28 x 20 cm) baking tin with good greaseproof paper or baking parchment. Lightly oil this.

Put the chestnut purée into a bowl, and beat in the brandy. In a separate mixing bowl, and using an electric whisk, beat the egg yolks, slowly and gradually adding the sugar. The yolks and sugar must be thick enough so that a ribbon-like trail formed by the whisk stays on the surface, and doesn't immediately sink back into the mixture. When all the sugar has been beaten in, combine this mixture with the chestnut purée.

Wipe out the mixing bowl and clean the beaters, then beat the egg whites to stiff, not floppy, peaks. Fold *half* of this into the chestnut purée mix, keeping the machine beating away at the egg whites, then fold in the balance. Turn out into your lined tray and gently push round into all the corners. Bake in the pre-heated oven for 15–20 minutes. Leave to cool.

When cold turn out of the tin on to a piece of silicone paper liberally sprinkled with icing sugar. Mix the whipped cream with the rum and 2 tablespoons of the icing sugar, then spread over the top of the roulade. Roll up carefully and gently, and place on your serving dish. Sprinkle with a little icing sugar.

CHOCOLATE WALNUT TORTE

A delicious cake topped with chocolate (for those who are addicted), which is as good when offered as a pudding as it is for tea or coffee time.

a little butter and plain flour for the tin

1 tablespoon white breadcrumbs

1 teaspoon ground cinnamon

1 tablespoon cocoa powder

5 eggs, separated

6 oz (175 g) caster sugar

6 oz (175 g) ground walnuts

2 oz (50 g) ground almonds

FILLING

10 fl oz (300 ml) double cream, whipped

2 tablespoons rum

1 tablespoon icing sugar

TOPPING

4 oz (100 g) plain chocolate, broken into small pieces

2 tablespoons rum

a walnut-sized knob of butter

Pre-heat the oven to 180°C/350°F/Gas 4. Grease and flour a 10 in (25 cm) round spring-sided cake tin.

Mix the breadcrumbs thoroughly with the cinnamon and cocoa powder. In a warm bowl, and using an electric whisk, beat the egg yolks until creamy, then slowly beat in the sugar, followed by the ground nuts and breadcrumbs. Beat the egg whites until stiff, not floppy, then fold into the yolk mixture.

Pour into the prepared cake tin and bake in the pre-heated oven for 45–60 minutes. Check after 45 minutes, and carry on cooking for another 15 minutes if you don't think it's quite ready. Remove from the oven and leave to cool.

When cold, split the cake horizontally. Mix the cream, rum and sugar together and spread over the bottom part of the cake. Top with the top half. Place on a serving plate.

For the topping, melt the chocolate with the rum in a double boiler, then stir in the butter. Pour over the top of the cake, and spread roughly.

BUTTERSCOTCH FOOL

Y ou can fool some of your friends most of the time with this infantile pudding! It's delicious.

6 fl oz (175 ml) Butterscotch Sauce (see right)

5 fl oz (150 ml) bought runny vanilla custard (or home-made, see page 187)

10 fl oz (300 ml) double cream

Put a teaspoon of Butterscotch Sauce in the base of each of four Manhattan glasses.

Beat together the remaining Butterscotch Sauce, the custard and cream and put into a piping bag fitted with a star nozzle. Pipe into the glasses then leave to chill.

BUTTERSCOTCH SAUCE

A stand-by in my fridge where it keeps well for a day or so. Use it to lift poached fruits or home-made ice-cream, or to add wonderful flavour to the 'fool' recipe on the left.

FILLS 2 X 1LB (450 G) JARS

1 x 1 lb (450 g) tin golden syrup

3 oz (75 g) butter

4 oz (100 g) soft brown sugar

5 fl oz (150 ml) double cream

a few drops of vanilla extract

Put the actual unopened tin of syrup into a small pan of hot water. This makes the syrup more runny and thus easier to get out of the tin.

Pour the syrup into a large thick-bottomed saucepan, and add the butter and sugar. Melt together very gently, stirring, and cook for about 10 minutes. Remove from the heat, cool a little, and then stir in the cream a little at a time, along with the vanilla. Stir until smooth, then use or decant into clean jars before storing in the fridge.

Butterscotch
Fool
(page 171)

Butterscotch
Sauce
(page 171)

Chestnut
Roulade
(page 169)

Chocolate
Walnut
Torte
(page 170)

TART LEMON TART

This tart can serve eight rather than four, but it lasts well, so you could save some for the next day's tea or supper!

1 x 8 in (20 cm) blind-baked pastry case (see page 114)

FILLING

2 lemons, quartered (preferably organic, as you use the peel)

10 fl oz (300 ml) dry white wine

8 oz (225 g) cube sugar

3 eggs

Pre-heat the oven to 180°C/350°F/Gas 4.

Poach the lemon quarters in the white wine with the sugar for 15 minutes. Remove the pips, and put the lemons, peel and all, in your food processor along with the syrupy wine mixture. Turn on to whizz at top speed, then add the eggs, one at a time, to blend thoroughly.

Pour the lemon custard through a coarse sieve into the blind-baked pastry case, and bake in the pre-heated oven for about 30 minutes. Serve warm or cold.

MY NAN'S TREACLE TART

An old favourite of mine, which my Nan used to make for me when I came home from school. It's very popular at Miller Howe. You could have prepared the pastry base well in advance (keep in an airtight tin), and then you can do the final baking just before your supper party.

1 x 10 in (25 cm) blind-baked pastry case (see page 114)

FILLING

4 oz (100 g) white breadcrumbs

5 oz (150 g) mixed cake fruit

½ teaspoon ground cinnamon

a good pinch of ground ginger

1 medium eating apple, cored and coarsely grated

juice and rind of 1 lemon

4 tablespoons golden syrup

2 medium eggs

TO SERVE

whipped double cream

Pre-heat the oven to 180°C/350°F/Gas 4.

Simply combine all the filling ingredients together in a mixing bowl, then spread into your baked-blind pastry case. Bake for 30 minutes.

Do not eat straight from the oven, but wait until the tart has cooled a little, then serve warm with the cream.

PATRICK'S IRISH CHOCOLATE CHEESECAKE

I am very lucky because, three years ago, Patrick opened his Irish restaurant just down the road from me, on the main Burnley Road. Food cooked with love abounds, and there is always a warm welcome. I invariably go for his Irish smoked salmon as a starter and follow this with chicken, but it is this pudding that gilds the lily. You could make it the night before, and chill until needed.

12 oz (350 g) good white chocolate (I use Sainsbury's), broken into pieces

5 tablespoons Bailey's Irish Cream

2 tablespoons Irish whiskey

15 fl oz (450 ml) crème fraîche

5 fl oz (150 ml) double cream, lightly whipped

BASE

8 oz (225 g) digestive biscuits, crushed

2 oz (50 g) butter, melted

Pre-heat the oven to 180°C/350°F/Gas 4.

For the base, combine the biscuit crumbs with the melted butter, and use to line the base of an 8 or 10 in (20 or 25 cm) round flan tin. Bake in the pre-heated oven for 20 minutes. Allow to go cold.

Sit a small pudding bowl over simmering water; the water must *not* be boiling, as white chocolate can be temperamental when melting. Add the chocolate and melt slowly, watching it carefully. Meanwhile warm your mixer bowl and wire whisks. As soon as the chocolate has melted, turn it out into the mixer bowl and start whisking *immediately*. Slowly dribble in the two lots of booze. It might look a bit funny, but have faith, it will stiffen and be smooth.

Fold in the *crème fraîche* and lightly whipped double cream, and then spread on to the cooked cooled base. Leave in the fridge to chill and set, at least 3 hours.

Tart
Lemon
Tart
(page 174)

Patrick's
Irish
Chocolate
Cheesecake
(page 175)

My
Nan's
Treacle
Tart
(page 176)

COMPOTE OF FRUIT WITH GRILLED ORANGE SLICES

You can serve this with a topping of Mascarpone and orange slices as a pudding or with natural yoghurt as breakfast – the latter is now on the breakfast menu at Miller Howe. Store any leftovers in the fridge. I also occasionally serve the compôte to accompany pavlovas.

4 oz (100 g) each of good quality dried apricots, prunes, figs and apple slices

1¼ pints (750 ml) boiling water

2 Earl Grey teabags

1 bottle cider of choice (about 9½ fl oz/275 ml)

1 sprig fresh rosemary

6 fresh sage leaves

TO SERVE

1 orange

butter

soft brown sugar

12 oz (350 g) Mascarpone cheese (optional)

Arrange the dried fruit in ever-decreasing circles or squares in a suitable dish – mine is about 7 x 5 in (18 x 13 cm) – finishing off with the apple slices over the top. Pour the boiling water over the teabags in a suitable container and leave for 5 minutes to infuse. Strain the hot liquid over the fruit. Cover the dish with cling film and leave overnight.

Pre-heat the oven to 180°C/350°F/ Gas 4, and pre-heat the grill to hot.

Strain the tea from the fruit and cover with the cider. Put the rosemary and sage on the top, cover with foil, and bake in the pre-heated oven for 1 hour. Leave to cool.

Meanwhile prepare the orange slices. Wipe the orange clean then cut into circles. Place on a buttered tray, paint with a little melted butter, and sprinkle with soft brown sugar. Grill under the hot grill for 5–8 minutes until they caramelise.

When the compôte is cold, remove the herbs. Pipe on the Mascarpone (if using), and top with the sticky orange slices.

FLAMED BANANAS

Basically a very simple dish, but it tastes wonderful and looks impressive, especially when flambéing. But *do* take care; although dramatic, it can be a little dangerous!

4 bananas

2 oz (50 g) butter

1 oz (25 g) demerara sugar

juice of ½ lemon

1 tablespoon water

2 tablespoons dark rum

TO SERVE

4 tablespoons fromage frais

Pre-heat the oven to 200°C/400°F/Gas 6.

Place the unpeeled bananas on a baking tray. Slit them down one side, three-quarters of the way, then bake in the pre-heated oven for 15 minutes. They will come out looking burned and a right mess.

Remove the skins and take out the banana flesh, whole if possible. In a frying pan large enough to take the four peeled bananas, melt the butter and sugar together over a medium heat, then add the lemon juice and water. Put the prepared bananas into this. Turn up the heat to full and pour in the dark rum. If you are lucky enough to have a gas burner, tilt the pan and light the rum (or simply use a match). Beware of the wonderful flames!

Serve at once with *fromage frais*.

FANNED RASPBERRY ALMOND MELON

You need to use ripe Charentais or Cantaloupe melons for this, which will be rich orange in colour and full of juice. The insipid honeydew melon just won't do at all. This fruity dish could also be served as a starter.

2 ripe small melons (see above)

1 oz (25 g) flaked almonds

RASPBERRY SAUCE

4 oz (100 g) frozen raspberries, defrosted

1 tablespoon brandy

1 tablespoon icing sugar

Pre-heat the oven to 180°C/350°F/Gas 4. Spread the flaked almonds on a flat baking tray, and bake in the pre-heated oven for 6 minutes. Leave to cool.

Cut the melons in half lengthways, through the stalk end, then in half again. Remove the skin, pips and inner garbage, then slice three-quarters of the way through so that each quarter of melon forms a fan. Put two fans on each chilled plate.

Liquidise the raspberries with the brandy and icing sugar to make a fruity sauce. Pour over the four fanned halves of melon and then scatter with the toasted flaked almonds.

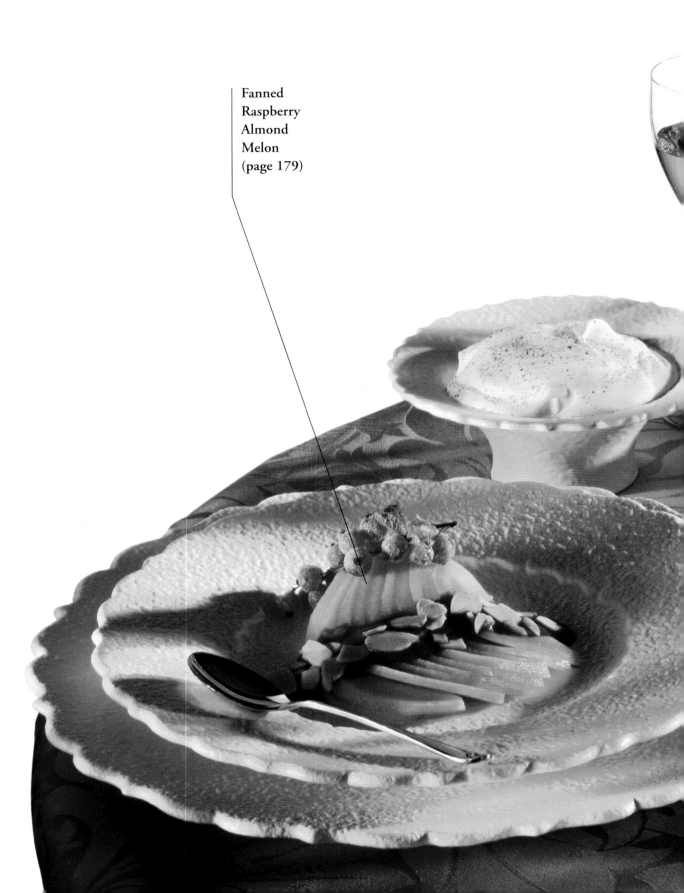

Fanned
Raspberry
Almond
Melon
(page 179)

Flamed
Bananas
(page 179)

Compôte of
Fruit
with
Grilled
Orange Slices
(page 178)

MINCEMEAT VIENNOISE TARTS

A nice variation on a seasonal favourite. I like mincemeat tarts and pies served with a brandy or rum butter, or they are good with ice-cream.

½ quantity Pie Pastry (see page 114)

6 oz (175 g) good mincemeat

icing sugar

VIENNOISE

4 oz (100 g) butter

1 oz (25 g) icing sugar

4 oz (100 g) plain flour

Pre-heat oven to 160°C/325°F/Gas 3, and have ready a twelve-hole mince pie tin.

Make the pastry, chill for 30 minutes, and remove from the fridge. When it has come round to room temperature again, roll out and use to line the mince pie tins. You don't need to leave any pastry for lids. Bake blind in the pre-heated oven for 15 minutes, then cool. When cold, fill with the mincemeat. Turn the oven temperature up to 180°C/350°F/Gas 4.

For the viennoise, beat the butter and icing sugar together well, then fold in the flour. Put into a piping bag fitted with a star nozzle, and pipe into blobs around the edges of the mince tarts. Leave a bit of the mincemeat showing.

Bake in the pre-heated oven for 20 minutes, then serve either warm or cold. Sprinkle with icing sugar.

DATE WEDGES

These go quite nicely with the Butterscotch Fool on page 171, and are certainly good for taking to work for elevenses. Make them a day or so in advance if you like.

4 oz (100 g) wholemeal flour

6 oz (175 g) porridge oats

8 oz (225 g) soft butter

8 oz (225 g) stoned dates, finely chopped

2 tablespoons rum

juice of ½ lemon

2 oz (50 g) soft brown sugar

generous ½ nutmeg, freshly grated

Have ready an 8 in (20 cm) square tin.

Combine the flour, oats and butter in a mixer, and beat until a softish dough is formed. Meanwhile simmer the dates and rum together with the lemon juice, sugar and nutmeg for 10 minutes. Leave to cool.

Spread half the dough mix into the tin, and put in the fridge to set. Spread the cooled date mix on top and once again put in the fridge to set. Top with the other half of the dough, and chill in the fridge yet again. All this could be done the night before.

When ready to cook, pre-heat the oven to 180°C/350°F/Gas 4. The tray will take 25–30 minutes to cook. Remove from the oven and, as cooling, turn out and cut into the size of wedges you wish.

SPICED BISCUITS

These biscuits are good to eat with your coffee after supper. Make at least a day before you need them.

4 oz (100 g) soft butter

4 oz (100 g) soft brown sugar

9 oz (250 g) self-raising flour

1 heaped teaspoon caraway seeds

1 heaped teaspoon ground cinnamon

1 large egg, lightly beaten

Pre-heat the oven to 180°C/350°F/Gas 4, and line a baking tray with good greaseproof paper.

Combine all the ingredients in your mixer, and beat to a dough. Roll out on a lightly floured work surface to ¼ in (5 mm) thick. Using a small cutter, make into circles. I used a cutter measuring 1¾ in (4 cm) in diameter, and made 26 biscuits. Place on the greaseproof paper lined tray, and bake in the preheated oven for 20 minutes.

As they are cooling, transfer to a cooling tray. Put into bags or an airtight tin only when stone cold.

Mincemeat
Viennoise
Tarts
(page 182)

Spiced
Biscuits
(page 183)

Date
Wedges
(page 183)

ZABAGLIONE SLICE

A delicious sponge dessert, using zabaglione as a filling. It will feed more than four guests, so you can enjoy some the next day!

SPONGE

3 medium eggs, separated

3 oz (75 g) caster sugar

3 tablespoons ground hazelnuts

½ tablespoon orange juice

finely grated rind of ½ orange

ZABAGLIONE FILLING

¼ oz (7.5 g) powdered gelatine

2 tablespoons Marsala

4 oz (100 g) caster sugar

3 medium eggs, separated

5 fl oz (150 ml) double cream

Pre-heat the oven to 180°C/350°F/Gas 4. Grease and line the sides and base of a 6 in (15 cm) spring-sided tin with good greaseproof paper.

For the sponge, whisk the egg yolks and sugar together in a warm mixer bowl until pale and thick, then gently fold in the ground hazelnuts, orange juice and rind. Beat the egg whites until stiff, then fold into the yolk mixture. Turn out into the lined tin and bake in the pre-heated oven for 20 minutes. Remove from the oven and leave to cool in the tin.

Halve the sponge horizontally and put one half back into the lined tin. For the filling, add the gelatine to the Marsala in a small pan and warm through *very* gently until the gelatine has dissolved. Meanwhile, whisk the sugar and egg yolks together in a warm mixer bowl until pale and thick. Add the reconstituted gelatine and whisk until well mixed.

In separate bowls, lightly whip the egg whites and double cream. Fold the cream into the yolk mixture first, then the egg white. Pour all this on to the sponge half in the tin, and place the other half of the sponge on top. Cover with cling film and refrigerate for 4 hours. Serve removed from the tin and cut into wedges.

VANILLA CUSTARD

You can, of course, *buy* perfectly good custard in cartons, but if you have time, there is nothing nicer than fresh home-made custard.

MAKES 10 FL OZ (300 ML)

3 medium egg yolks

1 tablespoon caster sugar

1 level teaspoon cornflour

½ teaspoon vanilla extract

1 tablespoon cooking brandy (optional)

5 fl oz (150 ml) double cream

5 fl oz (150 ml) single cream

Place the egg yolks, sugar, cornflour, vanilla and brandy, if using, in a large bowl and beat together until smooth.

Pour the two creams into a thick-bottomed saucepan and bring gently to the boil. Be careful that they don't boil over!

Pour the hot liquid on to the other ingredients and beat well together. Return the mixture to the saucepan, reduce the heat, and cook, stirring with a wooden spoon, until the custard starts to thicken. When ready, the mixture should coat the back of the spoon.

Strain through a fine sieve if there are any lumps, but there shouldn't be.

VARIATIONS

For an orange custard, add the juice and finely grated rind of 1½ oranges to the egg yolks. For a coffee custard, add ½ tablespoon Camp coffee essence to the egg yolks.

Zabaglione
Slice
(page 186)

Vanilla
Custard
(page 187)

Some Suggested Menus

MENU ONE
Savoury Mushrooms with Bolognese, Boursin
and Spinach (p.46)
Battered Monkfish (p.95) with
Mustard Dressing (p.21)
Chocolate Walnut Torte (p.170)

MENU TWO
Pepper and Onion Casserole with
Baked Egg (p.22)
Savoury Sole with Avocado and
Air-dried Ham (p.91)
Pavlova Roll (p.159)

MENU THREE
Dressed Spinach with Scrambled Eggs, Smoked
Bacon and Garlic Croûtons (p.22)
Marinated Cubed Salmon (p.82) on
Purée of Celeriac (p.146)
Sweet Pear Bake (p.166)

MENU FOUR
Chicken Liver Parfait (p.31)
Baked Pesto Cod (p.86) on
Baked Potato Circles (p.134)
Patrick's Irish Chocolate Cheesecake (p.175)

MENU FIVE
Prawn Cocktail (p.26)
Grilled Peppered Steaks (p.111)
Butterscotch Fool (p.171)

MENU SIX
Apple, Red Pepper and Sweetcorn
Cream Soup (p.15)
Casseroled Belly Pork with Pumpkin (p.108)
Cape Brandy Tart (p.149)

MENU SEVEN
Chilled Consommé Prawns with Sun-dried Tomatoes
and Crème Fraîche (p.26)
Peppered Orange Duck Breasts (p.103)
Fanned Raspberry Almond Melon (p.179)

MENU EIGHT
Aubergine Galette (p.35) on
Tomato Sauce (p.39)
Raised Pork Pie (p.107)
Rich Chocolate Cream with
Mascarpone (p.155)

MENU NINE
Aubergine Goat Cheese Custard (p.38) on
Tomato Sauce (p.39)
Mutton Pie with Chestnut, Watercress, Apricot and
Ginger (p.114)
Malva Pudding (p.168)

MENU TEN
Onion 'Flan' with Parmesan Eggs (p.51)
My Bolognese on Pasta (p.119)
Tangy Lemon Creams (p.154)

MENU ELEVEN
Fried Asparagus with Caper Butter Sauce (p.54)
Baked Garlic Chicken Breast (p.98)
Baked Curried Cream Pineapple
Meringue (p.163)

MENU TWELVE
Potted Prawns in Smoked Salmon (p.27)
Savoury Beef Olives (p.109)
Flamed Bananas (p.179)

MENU THIRTEEN
Egg Mayonnaise (p.19)
Roast Shoulder of Lamb with Garlic and Anchovies
(p.115)
Brown Betty Apples (p.166)

MENU FOURTEEN
Pasta with Sherried Dried Mushrooms (p.43)
Braised Lamb Cutlets with Garlic, Apple and
Rosemary (p.118)
Tart Lemon Tart (p.174)

Index

*Page numbers in italic refer to the
illustrations*

A

Almond Sauternes cake 150, *152*

Apples: apple, celery and mushroom soup 15

apple purée *120*, 122

apple, red pepper and sweetcorn soup *13*, 15

brown Betty apples *165*, 166–7

home-made chutney *41*, 42–3

Apricot stuffing *101*, 102-3

Asparagus: asparagus parcels *132*,
143

fried asparagus with caper
butter sauce *52*, 54

Aubergines: aubergine galette
35, *37*

aubergine goat cheese custard
36, 38–9

savoury rounds 62–3

B

Bacon: savoury rounds 64

Bananas: banana and parsnip soup
12, 14

filled pancakes 75, *77*

flamed bananas 179, *181*

Beef: grilled peppered steaks 111,
113

roast beef 110, *113*

savoury beef olives 109, *112*

Beetroot and orange soup *12*, 15

Biscuits, spiced *157*, 183, *184*

Black pudding with diced leeks
32, 34

Bolognese, my 119, *121*

Bread: cheese, chutney, garlic and
potato bread 66, *68*

savoury dinner rolls 66–7, *68*

Broccoli and cauliflower soup 15

Brussels sprouts, marinated, with
poppy and sesame seeds *144*,
146

Butterscotch fool 171, *172*

Butterscotch sauce 171, *172*

C

Cabbage: baked cabbage pizzas
124, 126

buttered caraway cabbage *128*,
143

deep-fried Savoy cabbage with
buttered eggs 23, *25*

Cakes: almond Sauternes cake
150, *152*

chocolate walnut torte 170, *173*

Cape brandy tart 149, *153*

Cauliflower, steamed, on tapenade
49, 50

Celeriac, purée of *144*, 146

Cheese: grilled Brie with Pernod
figs and Boursin *57*, 58

Cheesecake, Patrick's Irish chocolate 175, *176*

Chestnut roulade 169, *173*

Chicken: baked garlic chicken
breast *96*, 98

breast of chicken stuffed with
goat cheese, pineapple and
fennel *96*, 99

chicken broth with prunes and
bacon 18

roast chicken with Mascarpone, garlic, sage and orange
100, 102

savoury rounds 63

tropical chicken stir-fry *97*, 98

Chocolate: chocolate walnut torte
170, *173*

Patrick's Irish chocolate
cheesecake 175, *176*

rich chocolate cream with
Mascarpone 155, *156*

Choux pastry cups 65, *69*

Cod: baked pesto cod *85*, 86

cod with hot vinaigrette 82, *84*

Coeurs à la crème, meringue hearts
with *161*, 162

Cowboy trifle 151, *153*

Cream sauce *44*, 47

Crème brûlée, Earl Grey *156*, 158

Croûtons, savoury 64

Custard, vanilla 187, *188*

D

Date wedges 183, *185*

Duck breasts, peppered orange
101, 103

E

Earl Grey crème brûlée *156*, 158

Eggs: coddled eggs *17*, 20

egg mayonnaise *16*, 19

savoury rounds 64

scrambled eggs 23

F

Fruit compôte with grilled orange
slices 178, *181*

G

Garlic: garlic mayonnaise 21

garlic tomato dressing 21

H

Ham: filled pancakes 75

I

Ingredients 5–10

L

Lamb: braised lamb cutlets with
garlic, apple and rosemary *116*,
118

filled pancakes 74–5

mutton pie with chestnut,
watercress, apricot and
ginger 114–15, *117*

my Bolognese 119, *121*
roast shoulder with garlic and
anchovies 115, *117*
Leek with tarragon and cheese *124*,
147
Lemon: tangy lemon creams 154,
157
tart lemon tart 174, *176*
Liver: chicken liver parfait 31, *33*
fried chicken livers 30, *32*
lamb's liver with lamb's kidneys
120, 122

M
Malva pudding *165*, 168
Mayonnaise, quick 21
Melon, fanned raspberry almond
179, *180*
Meringue: baked curried cream
pineapple meringue *161*, 163
meringue hearts with coeurs à
la crème *161*, 162
Pavlova roll 159, *160*
Mincemeat Viennoise tarts 182,
184
Monkfish, battered *92*, 95
Muffins 71, *72*
Mushrooms: Irish farm mushroom
Roquefort 'baps' *45*, 46
mushroom caps in garlic cream
sauce *44*, 47
pasta with sherried dried
mushrooms *41*, 43
savoury mushrooms with
Bolognese, Boursin and
spinach *44*, 46
Mustard dressing 21

O
Olives: tapenade 50, *60*
Onions: balsamic onions *129*, 130
deep-fried pickling onions
131, *132*
onion 'flan' with Parmesan
eggs *48*, 51

P
Pancakes, filled 74–5, *76–7*

Parsnip and pear soup 15
Pasta with sherried dried mushrooms *41*, 43
Pavlova roll 159, *160*
Pear bake, sweet *164*, 166
Peppers: marinated 56, 59
pepper and onion casserole
with baked egg 22, *24*
savoury rounds 63
Pesto sauce 52, 55
Pineapple meringue, baked
curried cream *161*, 163
Pork: braised chops *105*, 106
casseroled belly pork with
pumpkin *104*, 108
raised pork pie *104*, 107
Potatoes: anchovy Parmesan new
potatoes *133*, 134
baked potato circles *128*, 134
curried cubed potatoes 135,
141
fried sliced garlic potatoes 139,
145
garlic puréed potatoes *137*,
139
soufflé baked potatoes *136*,
138
Prawns: chilled consommé prawns
with sun-dried tomatoes and
crème fraîche 27, *29*
potted prawns in smoked
salmon 27, *29*
prawn cocktail 26, *28*

Q
Quails' eggs, baked *17*, 20

S
Salade Niçoise 70, *72*
Salami rounds *40*, 42
Salmon: marinated cubed salmon
on purée of celeriac *81*, 82
salmon fishcakes 87, *89*
Sausagemeat: filled pancakes 75
Savoury rounds 62–4
Shallots, baked garlic coriander
131, *140*

Smoked salmon: savoury rounds
63
Sole: savoury sole with avocado
and air-dried ham 91, *93*
stuffed sole baked in cider *92*,
94
Soups *12–13*, 14–18
Spinach: dressed spinach with
scrambled eggs, smoked bacon
and garlic croûtons 22, *24*
filled pancakes 75, *76*
spinach and tomato soup 15

T
Tapenade 50, *60*
Tarts: Cape brandy tart 149, *153*
mincemeat Viennoise tarts
182, *184*
my Nan's treacle tart 174, *177*
tart lemon tart 174, *176*
Tomatoes: baked Mediterranean
tomatoes with pesto and Bel
Paese *53*, 55
filled pancakes 75, *76*
tomato sauce 39
Treacle tart, my Nan's 174, *177*
Trifle, cowboy 151, *153*
Trout: baked herbed trout 79, *80*
baked trout with almonds 79,
80
Tuna pasta 88, 90

V
Vegetables: barbecued vegetables
with Roquefort and pesto 56,
58–9
vegetable bake 123, *125*
vegetable spaghetti *141*, 142

Y
Yorkshire pudding with onion
gravy 70–1, *73*, *113*

Z
Zabaglione slice 186, *188*